Spreading the Word

Spreading the Word

EDITORS ON POETRY

Revised & Expanded Edition

Compiled by
Stephen Corey & Warren Slesinger

THE BENCH PRESS

04   03   02   01   5   4   3   2   1

The Bench Press
2507 Brighton Lane
Beaufort, SC 29902
slesin@islc.net

Grateful acknowledgment is hereby made to the editors of the magazines and
to the poets for permission to reprint the poems. The editors of this
anthology also ackhowledge the serial publication of the essays by Robin
Becker, Peter Cooley, and Dave Smith in *The Writer's Chronicle,* and the essay
by Marion K. Stocking in *Poets & Writers.*

Library of Congress Cataloging-in-Publication Data

Spreading the Word: Editors on Poetry/ compiled by Stephen Corey and
Warren Slesinger. – Rev. & Expanded ed.
   p. cm.
   Includes indexes.
ISBN 0–930769–15–5
1. Poetry–Editing. 2. Poetry–Publishing. 3. Poetry–21st Century–
2. History and criticism. I. Corey, Stephen, 1948– II. Slesinger, Warren.

PN1059.E35   S67   2001
070.5'1–dc21   2001-025305

Contents

❧❧❧

*Denotes works that appeared in the first edition

Introduction

"The word" of this anthology's original 1990 edition, featuring sixteen essays by editors from some of the country's leading literary journals, has spread slowly but steadily: *Spreading the Word* went out of print several years ago, but enough orders continued to come in that Warren Slesinger, publisher of The Bench Press and sole editor of the first edition, decided to create this revised and expanded version with the assistance of Stephen Corey, one of the original contributors. Fourteen of the twenty essays that follow are newly commissioned, while six are reprinted (most with variously modest alterations) from the first collection.

Because our essential plan for this new gathering remains what it was a decade ago, we think it fit that we repeat a portion of the first introduction:

> All of these editors discuss their personal editorial methods and their magazines' general philosophies; some remark on the overall state of writing, publishing, and reading in America. Each editor selects for complete reprinting here a poem that originally appeared in his or her magazine, a poem offered to the reader both for its own merits and by means of illustrating a range of points about editorial decision-making—including the relationship between the editor and the poet, problems encountered in the reading process, and the recognition of a truly outstanding poem.
>
> These essays will be of special interest to poets, teachers, other readers of poetry, enthusiasts for the essay form itself, and other editors of literary and nonliterary publications.

We see *Spreading the Word* as a rather unusual hybrid of the practical and the theoretical. Here, poets can glean information about the ways that different literary magazines handle manuscripts and can hear different editors' articulations of their philosophies and tastes. At the same time, poets and other readers can listen in on what amounts to a diverse forum concerning the nature of poetry itself and the art of reading poetry thoughtfully.

To help maintain this dual nature of the book, we have selected for reprinting from the first edition only essays that (1) are by editors still working with the magazines they wrote about a decade ago, and (2) seem to stand the test of time as essays, apart from their authors' particular affiliations. (In the table of contents we note with asterisks those works that appeared earlier.)

About one of the works retained from the original *Spreading the Word*, we must offer a sad addendum: Hale Chatfield, founder and then editor of *Hiram Poetry Review* for some thirty-four years, died suddenly on Thanksgiving Day, 2000, just as this book was moving into the final stages of production. Although the future of Chatfield's magazine is unknown to us as we write this, we have had no hesitation in our belief that his essay should be included here—for its intrinsic merits, which are of course undiminished by his passing, and also as a kind of memorial.

Concerning the fourteen new commentaries, we must offer a footnote on two: since the time that we commissioned and accepted the essays by Peter Cooley *(The North American Review)* and William Trowbridge *(The Laurel Review)*, each has ceased to be an editor for the publication about which he has written. We gave some thought to pulling these works from the collection since they no longer met our own announced criteria, but we soon decided that the expertise exhibited by these veteran editors—Cooley was with *The North American Review* for thirty years, Trowbridge with *The Laurel Review* for nearly fifteen—made their essays well worth keeping for the value of their broad insights.

Both conjunction and dissonance will be readily apparent to anyone who reads *Spreading the Word* in its entirety: a few poetic qualities, such as freshness of language and authenticity of voice, are mentioned frequently enough that they seem ready to wear the mantle of capital-*T* Truth and/or of cliché; but fisticuffs, verbal if not literal, would surely result if we could place these editors in a single room and ask them what they think of (for instance) making decisions by committee. Poets sending their work around should be heartened, we believe, by the fact that both consistency and inconsistency of opinion—dare we say "belief"?—are so alive and well on the other side of the symbolic transom.

Of necessity, the essays printed here represent only a fraction of the several hundred magazines that seem to be alive and tolerably well in the United States at this time. We had our sights on about another half-dozen pieces, but for one reason or another those did not work out. Some readers will note that we have included nothing from the new realm of electronically published periodicals, which scarcely existed when the first edition of *Spreading the Word* was being prepared. An unstated but not secret consideration in our selection process was the apparent stability of a magazine, often indicated by its longevity; because most poets like to think that the journals in which they publish will still be here in the foreseeable future, the usefulness of this anthology is to an extent pegged to that same quality of durability. E-zines may well be around to stay, and they could even prove to be the primary means of poetry publication at some time in the future, so a third print edition of *Spreading the Word* might of necessity include them—or perhaps an on-line anthology would be a more appropriate venue.

We have chosen to organize the essays in this edition according to the length of time each journal has been in continuous publication, beginning with the 109-year-old *The Sewanee Review* and concluding with two eleven-year-olds, *The Lesbian Review of Books* and *Many Mountains Moving.*

Our thanks to all the editors who have made this book possible, and also to the poets who have allowed their poems to be published here as integral parts of these essays.

Stephen Corey & Warren Slesinger
February 2001

Spreading the Word

The Sewanee Review

Founded 1892

The Antic Sound
of Mortality

George Core

In the more than twenty-five years that I have edited the *Sewanee Review*, I have regularly received many mindless inquiries, usually from people who are asking questions in order to avoid getting down to the job of writing, questions that often could be answered by a perusal of this magazine. I am reminded of an imperative statement that I saw on the copyright page of a quarterly well over thirty years ago which read: *Queries are not necessary.* I wondered about it then; I haven't since coming here.

Were I as curmudgeonly as Edmund Wilson, I would have a fierce statement printed on a card that runs along the lines of his famous blanket dismissal of persons whose questions and invitations and other demands upon his time offended him. If, on the other hand, I were possessed of E. B. White's genially satirical powers, I would have a different kind of card made up. The earnest soul seeking writer's guidelines would be instructed to hew to the straight and narrow, never to drink more intoxicating liquors than he or she could afford, to keep his or her underwear clean at all times, and so on. None of this would make the slightest difference, of course: the pointless inquiries would continue to come, just as they do now.

Real writers know, in general, what editors are looking for:

they know, without getting sketchy or elaborate instructions, what a given periodical of their acquaintance is likely to publish; and they know that anything good enough is likely to be accepted, even if it should violate various sacred guidelines.

I have, for instance, regularly inveighed against fiction exploring the geriatric theme. Since I have been here for well over half my misspent middle age, I have read hundreds of these stories, often little more than therapeutic exercises written by grieving people whose grief outruns their knowledge of fiction by a long measure. Finally, after six or seven years of rejecting these grim chronicles of old age—sickness, madness, death, defeat of every kind imaginable—I got a superb story about a plucky old man; and I published it. I did so in part because it had a comic and ironic element, a subtly orchestrated dimension in which the author satirizes the very subject that is being seriously presented in the story proper. Since then I have run at least three more stories dealing with old age, all by regular contributors. Before I lapse into senility myself, I may still again publish other stories about old people with lots of spunk and humor still left in them.

In 1989 I accepted a story about a preposterous situation: a widow of considerable breeding who is well-heeled and by no means mad or desperate marries an alcoholic hired man who had worked on her husband's ranch—and been fired—on more than one occasion. I find it hard to think of a more unpromising situation for a story than this, but the author, Christopher Tilghman, pulls it off. As Allen Tate used to say, a writer can do anything if he is man enough. (He did not say that to offend women writers, for he would have said the same of them—and to them.)

What I have said in general applies to poetry as well as fiction, it should go without saying. I have published many poems about far-fetched situations that, baldly described, would seem unpromising at best. Lately I have run poems about fruits and vegetables in the produce aisle, walking a blind dog, hunchbacks, the British Solomon Islands, stone walls in Ireland, aquifers, Thomas Wolfe, herb gardens, arrowheads, Monet, icehouses, Darwin in Rio de Janeiro, Pizarro, turtles, Wiglaf's life after *Beowulf,* various paintings and photographs, driftwood, peaches, old houses. Had I written a long instruction about the kinds of poetry that I am looking for, the likelihood is great that none of these subjects would have been mentioned. Again, if you are man enough or woman enough as a writer, you can find a subject that others think trivial or outmoded or even absurd and make it your own so thoroughly that a work of art results. If you are a real writer and are serious about your poetry or prose, you will get on with the job, no matter how grand or small, and not waste your time and an editor's by sending out inquiries. Can you imagine John Donne writing an editor and asking if he would be interested in considering a poem about compasses or the sun rising or riding westward on Good Friday? (Yes, the same chap who sees Donne publishing his work in a Penguin book has no difficulty envisioning Donne writing such letters.)

Now to hard cases–or one hard case. In 1983 or 84 Neal Bowers sent me a batch or two of poetry, and I took some of his poems, just as I have always taken at least one or two from every submission he has sent my way since that occasion. After pondering his poetry at some length, I observed that death seems to be his master theme. I was a little puzzled by this, for Bowers has a naturally sunny disposition and does not seem to be possessed by death in the fashion of, say, Donne or Laurence Sterne or Emily Dickson. I find it hard to see him as a pathologist or a mortician or even an obituarist; but such poems as "Driving in Greenwood Cemetery" and "Words for a fireman's Funeral" make it plain that although morbidity may not possess the dark corners of his imagination and haunt the inner recesses of his psyche, he is more than a little engaged by human mortality.

When I said as much to Mr. Bowers in a letter, he seemed taken aback, for he too did not think himself morbid by nature–and was perhaps a little upset by the prospect of anything so final as death. I should have thought Bowers solidly in the camp of Woody Allen, who has said that he is not afraid to die–only that he doesn't want to be there when it happens. But Bowers is committed to, if not a grimmer purpose, a larger design.

Looking back on this exchange and what resulted–namely "Notes from the Morticians' Convention"–he wrote this to me in a letter:

> Until your comment, I really hadn't been aware of how much and how often my poetic reflections turn to mortality, so I resolved to write the ultimate (and, I hoped, finally purgative) death poem.
>
> From the beginning, I wanted to have a poem that refused to take itself too seriously–not one that was frivolous or entirely comic, but definitely not one with muffled drums beating funeral marches to the grave. Howard Nemerov influenced me many years ago with a comment of his–something like "the serious and the comic are the same." They are, but it's not easy to point up their singleness, and the most difficult thing to attain in poetry is that fine balance between the laughable on the one side and the deadly serious on the other. Liking a challenge, I set myself the task of writing a seriously funny poem about death. Anyhow, it seemed an appropriate approach for a poem that was meant to be personally purgative, because it gave me an opportunity to make fun of myself and my "inclinations."
>
> Having never actually been to a morticians' convention, I simply modeled the convention structure after the Modern Language Association's annual meeting, and that gave me a chance to have another good, private laugh at the expense of a very serious organization. In all honesty, the MLA conventions are, for me, morticians' conventions–occasions for academicians to gather over the exquisite corpse of some obscure text. Again, though, I'm laughing at myself, because I've occasionally been right in there with the literary undertakers, embalming someone's corpus.

This wonderfully funny statement, with its reference to Nemerov, recalls Wylie Sypher's remark to the effect that comedy is a game that imitates life. In this instance life quickly turns toward death.– What else would be the subject of a morticians' convention? Our laughter suddenly begins to sound a little hollow as we confront the fact of our own mortality. Morticians can prepare us for being laid away. (Bowers has a poem about Aimee Semple McPherson, who was buried in a bronze casket, with a telephone at the ready, in case she literally received a call from the beyond.)

But they cannot prepare us for the final comedy that life seems to afford—that of redemption. Bowers neatly raises this question in terms of the pharaohs, not the up-to-date Christian who visits his late friends at the mortuary by going to a drive-in window.

The poem itself is modeled on the program of the professional convention, with subjects ranging from the profession's history (the oldest? the second oldest?) to its various methodologies. Naturally the mortician is perfectly modern in having methodologies, not methods, to follow; naturally he takes himself very seriously and finds time to dispel all the old jokes about his lack of ethics as he is thought, quite mistakenly of course, to violate the dead and to take advantage of them.

Carol Bly has written a grimly hilarious story—"The Dignity of Life"—about how a slick mortician sells coffins to the next-of-kin, always forcing the bereaved to buy a step or two above what the family can afford. Notice how Bowers moves up the ladder from the plain pine box to the ash and oak coffins.

Bowers has now almost played out his sophisticated joke that is based on the parallels between a morticians' convention and an MLA convention, a joke whose resonance echoes to the sacred precincts of the Princeton English club at which Allen Tate first presented "Miss Emily and the Bibliographer." There Tate worked out a complicated joke on literary historians; the joke was based on Faulkner's famous (infamous?) story, and of course it depended upon the expression the *corpus of literature.* Tate's punchline, you may recall, is this: "Miss Emily remains a somewhat endearing horror for me. It is better to pretend with Miss Emily that something dead is living than to pretend with the bibliographer that something living is dead."

There is one final turn of the screw in Bowers' poem, and it depends on the old Elizabethan pun about death—namely that one form of death occurs at the moment of sexual climax. The prostitute, whose name is Sybil and whose profession has been invoked in the opening lines, doles out "one small death / precise as stitchery." It is, like the convention itself and everything about morticians, a purely businesslike transaction and therefore devoid of life. As we think of this bloodless exchange of passion, other lines from the poem tease at our consciousness: "When you hear yourself say, / in a moment of passion, 'I love you more than life,' / think twice. Think twice."

The lines just quoted are the thematic culmination of the poem, a moment of passion in a passionless situation. But consider the poem for yourself:

Notes from the Morticians' Convention

9 A.M., Pine Room
"The Oldest Profession?"

> Whether the undertaker walked the street
> before the hooker, that is the question.
> Hard to tell in those early days
> of tree dwellers and cave sleepers,
> before a standard rate of exchange,
> even before barter.
> In the beginning, each gave what was needed—
> a warm embrace, a hole scratched in the ground
> and mounded with odd stones.
> This much is certain:
> death is older than life;
> life understands this and puts down
> unambiguous leaves.

10 A.M., Cedar Room
"Ethical Considerations in a Modern Market"

> To advertise or not, and if so how?
> Nobody skywrites any more.
> A billboard edged in black might be too gloomy.
> One small firm in Illinois canvasses parking lots,
> leaving fliers under wiper blades.

Another in Ohio uses direct mailings (more expensive).
For TV and radio you need a slogan:
We understand your needs or
Interment is our Business.
Of course there's always the Yellow Pages,
cheap and accessible to everyone,
a simple entry between Frozen Foods and Furnaces.

11 A.M., Pine Room
"Consoling the Bereaved: A New Methodology"

Grief is as varied as fish in the river,
sometimes small and visible in shallows,
sometimes large and mired in the bottom,
and everything in between.
The clever angler knows his fish,
knows also the currents of the river
and the river's snags and shoals.
He can cast between stumps near the far bank
or arc a fly out broad into the rapids,
play the line loose and easy or pull up short
to set the hook: mariboos, jitterbugs, trawlers and
crawlers,
and a special lure without a name
that must be tied in total darkness
at considerable pain.

Noon, Box Elder Grill
Lunch (Buffet Style)

Imagine a pharaoh rising in his pyramidal tomb
to eat the food left behind for his dark voyage
and finding kraut and wieners, green peas,
a gelatin salad, and a thermos of hotel coffee.
What better argument against an afterlife?

1 P.M., Oak Room
"Shrouded in Fear:
Some Popular Misconceptions Debunked"

> Death gives us no pleasure.
> Our hands are no clammier than anyone else's.
> We do not collect gold fillings.
> We do not steal jewelry.
> We never fondle the corpses.
> We know of no uses for the blood we drain.
> No one takes photos of the undressed women
> or wires a mouth to work like Charlie McCarthy's.
> We do not sell human hair to wig-makers.
> We care about our work the same as everyone else,
> some of us enough to write our names
> on a slip of paper and place it
> inside the coffin just before we close the lid.

2 P.M., Ash Room
"Billing and Collecting"

> Whatever else you do, do not make out the bill
> in the name of the deceased.

3 P.M., Oak Room
"Combatting Stress and Depression in Our Profession"

> Jog, golf, play tennis or poker,
> go out with the boys, swim,
> play pool, bowl, take in a movie.
> But don't raise canaries or gerbils.
> Collect shells or rocks,
> build model ships, paint landscapes,
> sculpt, surf, ski, go scuba diving.
> But do not dig worms, grow mushrooms,
> give blood, explore caves, or write poetry.

When you hear yourself say,
in a moment of passion, "I love you more than life,"
think twice. Think twice.

4 P.M., Grove Lounge
Cash Bar

That face in the mirror
hung over a short glass
like the moon embalmed, my own;
so many other drained faces,
so much gray and black—
I did not know death had employed so many—
all men, barbered and suited
and good at looking sympathetic
while their hands, manicured and pocketed,
brush against their genitals.
What this job needs is a woman's touch,
a woman then standing at each end of life,
twin gatekeepers saying hello-goodbye.

5:30 P.M., Room 3117
She said her name was Sibyl

Oracular blonde with the zippered skin—
tight slacks and hinged heels, as they say,
eyes dulled by the flat stop
of too many offwhite ceilings,
sipped exactly at her drink
on the end of the bed then
doled out one small death
precise as stitchery.
God, how we come and go—
selling hardware, selling software, selling death.
She folded the single bill and left.

I have no way of knowing whether the poem has become a part of the lore of morticians. It probably has not become a part of the dismal mythology of the Modern Language Association, for many of its members read little—and what they do read is inclined to lack the idiomatic exactness and complicated humor of "Notes from the Morticians' Convention." I do know that an alert editor at *Harper's* spotted the poem in the *Sewanee Review* and that it was soon reprinted in that magazine.

Bowers has since published a second book of his poetry. His original title, he tells me, was *Notes from the Morticians' Convention*, but lately he has changed it to *Night Vision*. The reason, he explains, is that "since several people whose judgment I trust told me that *Notes from the Morticians' Convention* created a morbid mood for them, even before they opened the book, I had to consider the possible liabilities inherent in such a title. . . . So I reluctantly made the change." Good old American squeamishness about death seems to have won out over our sense of humor. The joke in this sense has turned sour on the author. But the poem remains an endearing horror for me, a comic action of great force and subtlety whose playful rituals are deadly serious. We have to be dead not to relish the ironies and the humor in this splendid poem.

I now remount the hobbyhorse that I was riding when I began writing this essay. To the earnest and humorless reader who now asks if I am interested in receiving poems (or stories) about mortality, I would say Yes, for Bowers and the short-story writers to whom I have alluded (John Hazard Wildman, Helen Norris, Merrill Joan Gerber, William Hoffman) have not exhausted the subject by any means, although they have explored it in distinctive and memorable ways. What better way to measure and plumb the limits of our humanity than writing about our mortality? It is a great subject and a grand theme, but I would remind you that Dr. Johnson once observed that nothing is too little for so little a creature as man.

The themes of literary work, especially short poems, cannot always be grand and Miltonic. I think that writers should take to

heart what E. B. White said of himself seventy years ago: "I dis-
covered a long time ago that writing of the small things of the day,
the trivial matters of the heart, the inconsequential but near things
of this living, was the only kind of creative work which I could
accomplish with any sincerity or grace." The rewards of such en-
deavor," he continues, are that "I have occasionally had the ex-
quisite thrill of putting my finger on a little capsule of truth, and
heard it give the faint squeak of mortality under my pressure, an
antic sound."

The Southern Review

Founded 1936

A Few Sighs on the Subject of Editing, etc.

Dave Smith

Where I write today fall's last sycamore leaves are blown by wind that turns their infinite hues up to every angle of vision, and then turns them yet again. They appear to want to let go and yet they hold on. Some still have the full cheering green of summer in them. But some are already golden and there are rusty oaks nearby, and sycamores and spectacular maples whose burning red ripples and flashes as if it were designed to show us what's coming. The air is so cool that my fingers strike the keyboard just wrong. I, too, know what's coming. Even so, I want to be told, and told crisply, powerfully, with the weight of awful meaning, again and again.

That sense of weight, significance, power, scope, and, more than anything else, repeatability, is what I want in a poem, what I look for as an editor. When I accept poems, I always think such quality is there. But it is bosh to say that every poem I have published had all this. Often one's choices turn out to be provisional, erratic, or simply wrong, but you trust them. When I was in college and worked in a record store, a scruffy young face asked me to open and play a new album. I had been listening to Nancy Wilson and this new sound of the early 1960s was, I thought, beyond awful, scratchy and sullen and ghostly like the face I was startled to see on the album cover. I think it was fall, then, and I was certain he wasn't Elvis and wouldn't be ever. But I'd learn that one's rationale for choice changes: what was attractive isn't; what wasn't, becomes so. How much one's choices are explicable by objective standards of judgment, I cannot say. I know only that I choose what I like, and what I like seems to have some continuity.

An editor reads poems that appear before him or her. Most are rejected. Some editors, like Hollywood studio people, will make only a consensual decision. I heard a studio president make this joke: A writer asked me at a party what I thought of the script he had sent me. I told him I didn't know; a committee was reading it and hadn't yet told me what to think. I regard committees set up to judge poems as the consensual insecurity. Committees promote dullness in choices. The individual's choice, however, is usually idiosyncratic. I choose with no assist and no secondary reading from any other editor, an application of personal taste. But taste is a reflection of experience and temperament, of both firm and varying opinions. Younger writers and editors feel compelled to explain this in essays and statements that are often like tortured letters from a combat front. Older, one may throw up one's hands in acceptance and resignation.

Some editors say they want no cover letter to intrude on their judgment. They must be very malleable. I want a brief note which declares enough information to convince me the work is worth my reading time. If the letter tells me how much I will enjoy the material, gives me a plot summary, offers me serial rights, or mentions multiple submission, I reach for the author's stamped return envelope and I read no further. Editors have to find ways to avoid trash and to succor work that merits help and publication. Writers must learn competition for our pages is fierce and endless, and despite that we need them. Why do I reject? Here are some answers:

1) Writing is bad, conventional, sloppy, dull, dumb, offensive.

2) Writing is average; we have no time to teach improvement.
3) Writing is acceptable but subject is wrong for us: religious, political, etc.
4) Writing is good but spotty: subject undiscovered, unfocused, incomplete.
5) Writing is good, genre not for us: science fiction, detective fiction, romance.
6) Writing is good but we have done same subject in the last three years.
7) Writing is good but novellas take pages from other potential contributors.
8) Writing is good but we are doing a special issue of women, blacks, etc.
9) Writing is good but John Updike's, already in consideration, is better.
10) Writing is good but special circumstances obtain (budget, timing, sabbatical).

I know that I also reject poems for reasons that seem inexplicable, even unknowable, to writers. Perhaps it may help to say I am unmoved by poems without a story, a language of intensity and character, an interesting speaker, some matter of crisis in human endeavor. I don't like consciously arty poems; I am bored by poems overtly about poetry; I care little for poems that identify the rarity of their rare souls, that experiment with the keyboard as if no one had heard of e. e. cummings, that grasp my lapels with their righteousness. I have little time for Language poets, Bar-Bards, or Rapturists. I am equally immune to Polemicists who may or may not speak for righteous Angels who will greet us at the pearly gates.

Like all humans, poets learn most of what they do. They imitate. Editors see volumes of poems written as flash copies of Maya Angelou, Robert Hass, or Jorie Graham. Why not? Those people have the books, prizes, reading audiences, and public spotlight. We imitate far more than we write in our own voices. Any editor's toughest choice is knowing and finding those true poems by the author at hand. This is also the poet's labor. If the primary reason for rejection is the discovery that poems are just imitative, it is surely not the only reason. I edit two of four annual issues of our journal. I can use a maximum of 125 pages of poetry, 30 lines per page, or some two dozen poets per issue, forty-eight annually. Many write about the same things, as if simultaneously a zeigeist affects them. That it is good to vary the poets, to avoid repetition of subjects, treatments, and perspectives, seems to me obvious, and I may reject even what is of undeniable quality to avoid being redundant.

I reject because the poems seem unfinished. They too overtly echo their source writer; they circle their unrecognized but actual subjects. Some poems arrive with no subject, consisting only of language. Often this is the language of pretension or of raw matter, having all parts but one, like a laptop computer without a hard drive but otherwise intact and shiny. But worse is the poem whose subject, sometimes visible but more often latent, lacks intelligence, or what finally is individuality, is character. Were this poem a person, I would not socialize. Despite laudable attempts to be good citizens, some of us still think and behave like trolls—delightfully so. Poetry permits the examination of human behavior that finds one human worth time and attention and another not. In poetry, nothing is gerrymandered equal or equally acceptable.

Some editors avoid the poem that doesn't "sing." That lingo fouls too many sputtering brains. No poem sings. Sinatra did. The great divas do. Poems talk. Still, it is talk of a dialectical character which lodges in and compels and provokes us, talk made of rhythmical sounds. The rhythm of a poem is the voice of character and is as real as the human voice inside all of us. No rhythmic voice, no poem. Yet people send us a species of discourse, visually idiosyncratic, which apparently must give sonic pleasuring, a lyric glossolalia, to some readers. To such, I am indifferent. There are writers who prefer comic books to Joyce. Their poems reflect this and I dutifully reject these. I find no value in artifice if a poem's human voice doesn't memorably, referentially, and compellingly speak. I frequently reject verse that is only a game of syllabic patterns and easy statements, an adornment of style. All poems should be composed to bring forth an inevitable, necessary talk. Nothing is more public, more artful than this, nothing less merely individual. I believe Stanley Plumly has illustrated the nature of a poem's obligation, carried by rhythm, when he says of an ending: the poem must weigh more at the bottom than at the top.

Any citation of do's and don't's makes only a rough template of what my experience has shown me to look for or away from. I often reject gimmicks which are affectations, the visual do-dah of the keyboards, indulgent typographies, titles waterfalling into poems, the insistent small-*i* pronoun, a lack of punctuation, a refusal to capitalize properly. (Do you not wonder, reader, if such writers insist on small-capping a driver's license, a checkbook, a mortgage document?) I am wary of epigrams, of elliptical, floating parts, spatial wallpapering, and poems whose sentences could not help me around a sudden doggy pile. I distrust droning phrases of self-exposition, appositive catalogues of intense sensitivity, wails (whales?) of feeling. I feel cornered by poems about painters, painting, and sculpture wherein the certified metaphor of art comes so readily to hand the poet need only whine his nearness and dearness.

* * *

If so much constitutes what I avoid, what then do I seek? To answer asserts a formula I do not have. Statements of what editors want make me cringe in despair. They sound like bad poets: "the challenging, fresh, socially committed," "the durable, the beautiful." It makes me long for W. C. Fields, even Jerry Seinfeld's yadda, yadda, yadda. If an editor knows so precisely what he looks for, if he knows what he wants, you won't want it. It's already packaged, dried. Do we need another *Waste Land*? The unwritten and unpublished poem is immensely harder to imagine, to describe, than those we don't want, but we are not halted in trying to know, and to say, what we editors think. Our choosing, like the poet's writing, manifests an appetite for the real and abundant shapes of our lives. I seek the poem that resists and fulfills our destiny.

Readers recognize that sifting through voluminous mail is often a serendipitous search for treasures. I know *Poetry* magazine has an annual submission that would stagger teams of readers, though I do not know their numbers. It may be they record what they receive. *The Southern Review* does not. Poems arrive addressed to me, to coeditor James Olney, and to The Editors. Olney and I read, individually, what comes to us; an associate reads the rest, and he passes on what he regards as worthy of our attention. Little gets beyond him. I suppose we receive in excess of twenty thousand poems annually. Maybe more or less. And yet, and yet, as editors know, many poets we read and admire do not send us their poems. The reasons are not hard to see: poets in demand send work to journals who ask for it, typically journals with good circulation, decent payment, handsome presentation, and the best competitor poets. To get these, we correspond and telephone mightily. We ask for poems we hear read in public. We try to establish a relationship of loyalty and gratitude, hoping for reciprocity, and we are apt to publish some poets repeatedly (thus cutting spaces for others). The best poems are the endgame. I keep no records about the proportion of poems I take from solicitation or from transom receipt, but either without the other, I am convinced, would hardly make a readable magazine.

Any good journal begins with editorial recognition of potential, but editors need to do nurturing work after that. Too often they do not. The best, like *The New Yorker's* late Howard Moss and *The Georgia Review's* late Stanley Lindberg, pay close and gentle attention to what might make the poem better. This can be summed up in a demand for clarity. Editors want the poem to speak as clearly as it can, its vocabulary appropriate and right, its diction and tone transmitting, its sentences sinuous, alive, bearing the goods forward, its scene fully staged, its actors visible and sonorous, its plot functional, followable, and complete. The single most difficult labor for clarity is to reveal and make shapely what only the poem knows, that matter we abuse a little when we call it *meaning.* Clarity, as I intend it here, refers to functional simultaneity, the parallel livingness of secondary things and first or paraphrasable contents. We can say with confidence that Keats's "Ode to a Nightingale" is about a bird and a watching man. But we know it is about much less categorical matters, much more layered and impalpable things on a secondary level. The editor always negotiates between degrees of clarity at both levels, but he must not and cannot function as reviser of the poem. That is the danger for the Hollywood screenwriters and for the committee decision. Nevertheless, the editor's best work lies in fulfilling a poem's potential. Oddly enough this sometimes means negotiating the insecurities of poets. While loath to forgo their work, I do so in the face of problems not easily resolved. I have found that, without exception, the most experienced writers—Lee Smith, Russell Fraser, Robert Penn Warren—were most eager to revise to whatever extent I asked.

So what poem would I choose to illustrate my own editorship? Is it to be one I bent over, with the poet, to find that better clarity? No, because that diminishes the author, however much I might wish to think myself a helpmate. And what could I say to the poem which came, as Frost says, like a gift, all itself and all as we'd want it? Only that this is a gift one willingly chooses and that thereby expresses, implicitly, all worth saying of one's editorial taste. That is why I tell people who write to me for editorial guidelines to read an issue and see for themselves. So, among the many poems I've chosen and printed, there is little reason to single out "Shiloh" by the late Larry Levis, except that I find it startling, charming, witty, macabre, cautionary, and a good entertainment. Here it is:

Shiloh

When my friends found me after I'd been blown
Into the limbs of a tree, my arms were wide open.
It must have looked as if I were welcoming something.

Awakening to it. They left my arms like that,
Not because of the triumphant, mocking shape they took
In death, & not because the withheld breath

Of death surprised my arms, made them believe,
For a split second, that they were really wings
Instead of arms, & had always been wings. No, it was

Because, by the time the others found me, I had been
Sitting there for hours with my arms spread wide,
And when they tried, they couldn't bend them back,

Couldn't cross them over my chest as was the custom,
So that the corpses that kept lining the tracks
Might look like sleeping choirboys. They were

No choir, although in death they were restored
To all they had been once. They were just boys
Falling back into the woods & the ravines again.

I could see that much in the stingy, alternating light
And shade the train threw out as it began to slow,
And the rest of us gazed out from what seemed to me

One endless, empty window on what had to be.
What had to be came nearer in a sudden hiss of brakes,
The glass clouding with our reflections as we stood.

Arms & wings. They'll mock you one way or the other.

"Shiloh" isn't Larry Levis' best poem, but I could get his poems only occasionally and I thought it distinguished enough. Still, it had to overcome prejudices in me. The original editors of *The Southern Review*, Robert Penn Warren and Cleanth Brooks, were writing the literature of the American South, a thing done so well by William Faulkner it had an international life. These editors were determined not to be or to appear parochial. Writing about the South per se evoked quick rejection unless the writing demanded otherwise. This remains our editorial position. Work about Louisiana is especially suspicious to us. Yet if we are anti-regionalist, we are drawn to our heritage and its making, and to nothing more than the Civil War. Levis, a native of California, has made a poem about one of the battles that made us Americans. Without identifying the speaker's army, Levis adopts the voice of a battlefield corpse stricken with rigor mortis and waiting for transport by a casualty train. In the line "They were just boys. . . ," Levis evokes Herman Melville's scathing indictment of war's results, but Levis contains, perhaps I mean sustains, our interest by writing not antiwar polemic, not a regionalist advocacy, not even a pro forma protest against dreadful death. Instead, he laments the failures of the body and through that the fate that mocks us all "one way or the other." I admired, and still admire, the rhythmic surge of the long sentence, the pause for a crisply short one, then a looping forward—this is a good dancer, poised and confident in execution, one who surprises and delights and, at the final unraveling instant, instructs. This is artful work.

How does any reader, all an editor is, know that the arrangement of words and lines upon the page is, in fact, a poem? How does the poem achieve a signature of success which begins, but hardly ends, in imposition of left-hand margins, clusters of lines, line breaks, and language with figurative function? *That* the reader, the editor, decides, which opens all the spookiest doors of the castle. By as much as Levis subverts form, displaces and remounts expectations on the uncertain footers of what we know, he pushes us through old experience. His poem speaks from the interior, lyrical, anecdotal, obsessive. It celebrates the near death of speech, where we exist or do not. It renews poetry where I least expected or thought to find it. The poem asks me to redefine what poetry is and might be—like that face asking me to play a record so long ago, one that would turn out to be the song bard of our times, Bob Dylan. I thought what he caused me to hear wasn't music, just an awful, raspy, ratcheting anthem of some undesirable cousin. Now, when I hear only a few notes of "Blowin' in the Wind" my heart beats with sudden intensity, with the kind of recognition that a poem can deliver. But if "Blowin' in the Wind" were a poem I'd have rejected it, publishing "Shiloh" instead. All I know about editing is that you listen, you choose, you print it. Maybe you get lucky enough to have good readers.

The Kenyon Review

Founded 1939

Conjure: An Editor's Momentary Pause

David Baker

To conjure means in its original form to swear together—as in a private alliance—or to conspire, which itself means to breathe together, to whisper in secret. It bears more than a touch of magic and subversion, a hex: enchantment. The thing conjured is potentially dangerous, but it can also be healing, even transformative, a paradox.

For nearly twenty years I have conjured the poem. I have sat down in my chair, in offices in Salt Lake City, in Gambier, Ohio, and now in Granville, Ohio, and opened tens of thousands of envelopes packed with poems and letters and self-addressed stamped return envelopes. I have conjured my hope and patience and best imagination, searching for brilliance, discipline, and the flash of subversion and conspiracy which good poetry demands.

I have wanted to be an editor since I began seriously to write. To edit seemed to me, and seems now, a way to participate in a big, rowdy conversation among writers and readers. It is an honorable way to belong to the loose but long-lived community of people who believe in the value, and who feel the urgent need, of rigorous, inventive language. It is my good fortune to have been able to serve for this long. I have worked primarily for two literary magazines—*Quarterly West* and *The Kenyon Review*—though like many of us I have also been a consultant or advisor or reader for several other magazines and presses.

When I moved to Salt Lake City in 1979 to pursue my Ph.D., one of my first exploratory ventures was to visit the offices of *Quarterly West.* Staffed wholly by graduate students, supported by the University of Utah only with office space (tiny, crammed), the magazine was itself a paradox: highly regarded outside of town and yet barely noticed, more a shambles than an institution, at home. I began as proofreader for that year's only issue, edited by Terry Hummer. I was giddy. I checked blue-lines and compared proof to the fine, folded work of other people's manuscripts. I continued in 1980 as poetry editor, then from 1981–1983 as editor. We received lots of manuscripts, few subscriptions, little local encouragement.

In 1983 I took my first college teaching position at Kenyon College in Gambier, and while I stayed at Kenyon only for a year (I've been at Denison since then, twenty-five miles down the road), I have maintained an editorial association with the magazine ever since. Again, my titles and duties have evolved, even as the editor's position has evolved. In these fifteen years the magazine's editors have been Philip Church and Galbraith Crump, Terry Hummer, David Lynn (interim), Marilyn Hacker, and now, permanently, David Lynn; my own positions have been editorial assistant (Church and Crump), assistant editor (Hummer), poetry editor (interim, Lynn), consulting poetry editor (Hacker), and now poetry editor (Lynn). The tastes and visions of these talented people sometimes overlapped, sometimes did not, and the magazine has prospered and deepened under each person's stewardship. I am proud that *The Kenyon Review* is a magazine I want to read.

All this is to say, I have become a poetry editor by a kind of haphazard evolution and a conviction about doing the abundant work at hand. My experience tells me that's how literary magazines and magazine editing work these days. It's not a mystery: literary magazines are typically staffed by a very few people (often unpaid, or poorly so) who do an ungodly amount of work, only part of which work involves reading, selecting, and editing manuscripts.

At two different writers' conferences recently, I conducted a number of consultations and gave talks about editing. Some of the many questions were familiar ones. How do I feel about simultaneous submissions? I hate them; don't do it; you'll go to Editor Hell. What should cover letters cover? They are unimportant, and should be brief and to the point. Why does it take so long to hear from magazine editors these days? Because the numbers of manuscripts have burgeoned in relation to the numbers of simultaneous submissions and the very large enrollment in graduate writing programs. And because we try to be careful, and attentive, and make good choices.

What happens to a manuscript when it comes in? It enters the office (usually by mail, sometimes by stealth) where it is logged in, carefully, then routed to a reader. Sometimes that reader is a Kenyon faculty member. Sometimes it goes straight to me or to David. If it is fiction or nonfiction, and goes to a screener and passes muster, then it is forwarded to David with commentary (sometimes extensive, sometimes bare-bones); if poetry, to me. David makes the final decisions about everything and sends those happy notices of acceptance to everyone himself, although with poetry his final decision is almost always what I've suggested.

Yes, sometimes we solicit work or writers. Why? It's easy to get good work; it's hard to get the best.

And still other questions, good-willed and clear, left me unable to give good answers. What is our policy toward poetry? I gave a rambling response; and later, when I asked David, he said "We're for it." What kind of poetry do we favor? "Good poetry," I said, then regretted my answer, too quick and empty. But here is where it gets hard. What do I favor? I do not like short poems more than long ones; I am pleased that *The Kenyon Review* reserves quite a bit of space, as needed, to feature longer poetic texts. I cannot say that I prefer narrative poems, or lyric poems, or meditative poems, or political poems. As soon as I might say so, then all the beautiful exceptions come calling forth. I prefer one poem at a time. In fact, I am awfully suspicious of such modal labels these days—not that they aren't meaningful, but that they are too readily misunderstood or too naively applied. I am also suspicious of magazines or editorial tastes which privilege these modes too highly. An example: I do like narrative exploration and experimentation in poetry, and at the same time, the single most boring component or movement in contemporary American poetry is "narrative poetry," especially that plodding, chronological, traditional narrative, which traces a poet's (okay, a speaker's) experience and results in a little epiphany, where that speaker's experience is emblematic of ours. Sigh. Or where the ending is merely a tidy tying-up of the one or two plot threads introduced earlier. Or where the sun sets.

I do not like to be confused on purpose, though I have bountiful patience (with myself as well as with a text) to work with the difficult, when I sense genuine exploration. I distrust poems that ought to have been graduate school papers in philosophic discourse. I distrust religious verse, the too-private, the merely didactic, the nifty, the poem-as-riddle, the too-familiar. But mostly I disbelieve the poorly written, and refuse it out of hand.

What I like is to be surprised and reoriented, to be retrained by a poem in how to read a poem. I like poems that resist the ready categories above, that seem to stand both inside and outside, and make a category for themselves. I like risk and danger, radical music, rigor of feeling, subtlety, noise, technical grace, crafty daring.

I remember vividly when I opened the envelope, from Robert Wrigley, which contained the following poem, "Conjure." I've been a fan of his since 1979 when his *The Sinking of Clay City* first appeared. His work has continued to deepen and clarify; he's one of the many to whom I look. In this envelope were several splendid poems, and we printed two others. But this one—. Well, take a look.

> There is nothing of her body he can't
> conjure—texture, heft, taste, or smell.
> This is heaven, and this is also hell.
> He can dream the way moonlight comes slant

through the window, illuminating breast
and breast, her navel a shadowy pool
he drinks the darkness from, her skin grown cool,
and her lips and her lips and all the rest.

If she were here, he thinks, and he thinks too
much, he thinks. He thinks too much when she's here,
and when she's gone. And the window's a mirror
he's not alone in. If he could say he knew

every night would be made of her, a thigh
in the true air, her long, elegant spine
blossoming forth from the clothes on the line,
he would have asked, he would have asked her why

the sigh of the evening breeze is her tongue
and the rose of her cast-off shirt his hand
unfillable and trying. He can stand
and go and find her still-damp towel among

the morning's last mementos, and the shape
of her ear, a whorl on the pillow's white.
He can feel the whole weight of her at night
and the weight of her absence, and her hip.

He would say when she's gone he loves too much.
He's immoderate or reckless. He cries
and laughs at his crying, his dreams are lies
he cannot live without, a drunk, a lush,

inebriate of skin and bone and hair.
But reason has no mouth to kiss, no eyes
he dives in. His head aches. He is not wise,
but strokes the round, blue corporeal air

and conjures her painfully into place.
Most chaste of lovers he is, a shadow

man enamored of another shadow,
and the dark he is kissing is her face.

It struck me quickly that Wrigley rarely writes in syllabic qua-
trains, and not often in perfect rhyme. Yet in this poem these for-
malizing factors assert themselves quickly. So do the echoes. I
must have cringed a little on hearing "Hotel California" in line
three; I like the Eagles, too, but I see so many poems whose *only*
allusive pursuit is rock-and-roll. That Dickinsonian "slant" of light
in the next line appealed quickly and clearly, ironizing the pre-
vious allusion. How could one not notice that "slant," since it is
such an adverbial oddity and since it is highlighted by the stanza
and line enjambment?

The narrative of the poem is lucid and evident. The lone lover
imagines his partner, and his subsequent dream, his reverie, is in-
toxicating and freeing. He sees in his mind their love-making, he
wills it, he makes it. He "thinks" it. The sensual detail—and sen-
sory variety—increases until he seems actually to "feel the whole
weight of her" as he begins to "[stroke] the round, blue, corpo-
real air." The pleasures are abundant, but not wholly pleasant. In
fact, his freedom is not liberating at all, and this paradox is one
of the poem's smartest tropes. The crazy repetitions provide a
tangible uneasiness—dizzy, confused, "immoderate": "If she were
here, he thinks, and he thinks too / much, he thinks. He thinks
too much when she's here, / and when she's gone." Too much
thought leads to other excesses: "He would say when she's gone
he loves too much." To love too much is great pain indeed. The
prior reckless or abandoning commotion has intensified until,
here in stanza seven, he issues a catalog of miseries, intoxicated
by a kind of guilt and by the fear of solitude, the fear of "her"
absence.

Masturbation may be one of the purest forms of self-pleasure,
though we are taught its shame: the poem's paradox. Isolate, it is
also a connective gesture, as when "the window's a mirror he's
not alone in." One becomes, as one "thinks" of, two. It expresses
need. It may also be a form of solace or retreat, our comfort. It
may soothe—even as it provides—our pain. I admire the un-

abashed directness of the poem, the depth of its complexity. It goes where few poems go, and it goes as art, not as mere confession, self-exploitation, or exhibition.

But there is more. If Dickinson's light slants through the window in stanza one, and gives us a prefiguration of "Heavenly Hurt"–that companion paradox, where we "find no scar"–then I find a more pertinent and consequential Dickinson echo in the eighth stanza of Wrigley's poem. Recall these lines from her "I taste a liquor never brewed": "Inebriate of Air–am I– / And Debauchee of Dew– / Reeling–thro endless summer days. . . ." The richness of Wrigley's painful, more bodily pun, "inebriate of . . . hair," indicates again the doubleness of his strategy. He's having a lot of fun even as it hurts. Notice how the stanza's final "air"– again, pointedly enjambed and perfectly rhymed with "hair"–also points further back to Dickinson's "Air."

The very air she breathes provides Dickinson a transporting "dram." She languishes in the sensory richness of her imagination, where flowers and bees are her company. The saintly, distant townspeople must "to windows run" to see her risen so large she can "[lean] against the–Sun." Just so, Wrigley's darker room has provided a place where the imagination–clearly phallic–can "stand and go." Notice, too, how this connects with Yeats's Innisfree, where he will "arise and go now" to that better, imagined garden to "live alone in the bee-loud glade." Yeats is more peaceful and Dickinson more spirited; yet, just as they do, Wrigley locates an erotic and transporting capacity inside the lyric, constructing an alternate place for the imagination to reside. Such artistic space is the "dream" and the "lie" we "cannot live without." His speaker is as tormented as delighted, no doubt. But remember, he is himself also "a shadow man," a figure in a poem, a trope of his own desire and design.

What I mean is this: The intense self-interest embedded in Wrigley's poem is–the primary paradox–its most vivid point of connection, allusion, and contact. It is both example and parable of the lonely public history of the lyric poem. It is beautiful, and it is smart.

The Georgia Review

Founded 1947

A Squirming Aleph:
On David Swanger's
"What the Wing Says"

Stephen Corey

In a way that is rare even among the finest of poems, David Swanger's "What the Wing Says" seems to speak about nearly everything by remaining open to an astonishing range of possibilities. Whenever I read it I am challenged, pleased, mystified, satisfied—and I am always led to recall "The Aleph," a tale by Jorge Luis Borges. An aleph is "one of the points in space containing all points," a mythical / magical spot where, "without any possible confusion, all the places in the world are found, from every angle." Swanger's poem is not so perfectly complete and balanced that it could qualify as a true aleph, but I find the comparison crucial for arriving at any statements about this poem, which moves me in such a way that I am almost speechless in its presence.

What the Wing Says

The wing says, "I am the space behind you,
a dent in the fender, hands you remember
for the way they touched you. You can look

back and song will still throb. I am air
moving ahead, the outermost edge of desire,
the ripple of departure and arrival. But

I will speak more plainly: you think you are
the middle of your life, your own fulcrum,
your years poised like reckonings in the balance.
This is not so: dismiss the grocer of your soul.
Nothing important can be weighed, which is why
I am the silver river of your mornings and
the silver lake curled around your dark dreams.
I am not wax nor tricks stolen from birds.

I know you despair at noon, when sky overflows
with the present tense, and at night as you lie
among those you have wronged; I know you have failed
in what matters most, and use your groin to forget.
Does the future move in only one direction?
Think how roots find their way, how hair spreads
on the pillow, how watercolors give birth to light.
Think how dangerous I am, because of what I offer you."

When I was an undergraduate, I wrote a brief essay declaring how
the perfect poem would elicit only silence from the right reader,
who would understand implicitly that any attempted discussion
would result in a lessening both of the poem and of the reader's
appreciation for it. I suspect now that at the time I was trying to
seem clever and sensitive, as well as to avoid any rigorous think-
ing and writing; I also suspect that I was closer to being right than
I could have known.

Not quite so many years ago, under duress of the job-seeking
process, I was required to formulate a one-page statement of the
qualities of excellent, publishable writing. In a rare instance of
hard-thinking good fortune, I brought to the surface some usu-
ally unarticulated grounds for what feel like my visceral reactions
to literature—although they have been influenced, unavoidably,

by my lifetime of reading and study. I compressed my opinions into five points, applicable in differing balances to all genres: physically pleasing flow of language, fresh metaphor, connection with the ongoing human world, wholeness of the particular imaginative realm created, and surprise (including, though not necessarily, the absence of one or all of the first four elements).

To name these components is not to be able to explain all of my editorial choices in their light, nor is it to say I could mechanically match these qualities with pieces of writing in some objective way. We speak of "editorial taste," and I believe *that* metaphor is a vitally apt one. All of us have many favorite foods and dishes that we "love" in varying ways and to different degrees. So, in certain regards, with poems. Every poem I would choose to publish must gain a certain baseline commitment from me: the poem must seem new in its language (and, if I am doubly lucky, in its content as well), so that the work strikes me as being not quite like any of the tens of thousands I have seen before; the poem must make me believe I will continue to be enthralled by it in the future, and that many readers of my magazine will be similarly, permanently held; and the poem must drive me to feel that I cannot let it get away, cannot let another editor be the one to bring this particular excellence before the public.. But, as I said, these are the minimum requirements, with each element noted being capable of substantial intensification. I can't imagine any editor having equal love for all the work he or she publishes.

"What the Wing Says" captivates me immediately, offering through its arresting title the prospect of a strange world–even before I have begun to read the poem proper. The twenty-two lines are then delicately relentless in their fostering of this strangeness, managing to keep me completely off kilter yet dead on line. The seemingly symbolic / surrealistic imagery is toned down to an extent by the poem's soothing and quite regular music, dominated by forward- tumbling anapests and iambs. The lines have a basic range of ten to twelve syllables, with "irregulars" containing nine, thirteen, and fifteen. The lines grow gradually longer as the poem develops, but in a way whose effects never intrude themselves. Accentually, the lines cluster around five and six primary beats–with, again, more fives near the beginning and more sixes toward the end.

Thus, the poem adheres to no traditional form, yet its prosody is anything but random or "free." The factors I've just quantified produce a strong frame that partially contains the elusive proposals of the wing:

> "I am the space behind you,
> a dent in the fender, hands you remember
> for the way they touched you. You can look
> back and song will still throb. I am air
> moving ahead, the outermost edge of desire,
> the ripple of departure and arrival. But . . ."

Here, Swanger's aleph offers hints about danger, damage, memory, sensuousness and love, the future and possibility, persistence and contradiction. We are held in suspension by this odd tumble of declarative statements, swept ahead by this nearly deranged–yet authoritative–voice. And the intelligence of the voice appears to include its awareness that we can only take so much of this unusual cataloging: at stanza's end, the wing appears to shift the winds, to negate everything in the preceding half-dozen lines with that concluding "but." The wing is not just a lyricist, it is a polemical philosopher as well:

> "I will speak more plainly: you think you are
> the middle of your life, your own fulcrum,
> your years poised like reckonings in the balance.
> This is not so: dismiss the grocer of your soul.
> Nothing important can be weighed . . ."

We may well breathe a small sigh of relief upon hearing that our tenuous position in stanza one will be solidified, even though we must endure being chided for selfishness and a mean-spirited outlook on existence. This lecturer even exhibits a previously hidden sense of humor, undercutting his own preachiness with the one-liner about metaphysical grocers.

A larger sense of humor is at work here also, the one that knew speaking "more plainly" was a ruse because there can be no such approach. The first half of stanza two is merely an interlude, a relenting, prior to the rush of curious beauties that will carry us to the poem's end: "'I am the silver river of your mornings and / the silver lake curled around your dark dreams.'" A new beginning possible with each day, the counterpointing of nightmare with hope—such are the "facts" that spring from the abandoning of the false scales.

Possibility and hope: these emerge more and more persistently as the poem continues. We hear at the conclusion of stanza two what we already have sensed—that this voice is alive and honest ("I am not wax nor tricks stolen from birds"). At the start of the third and final stanza, we realize the wing is not only around us (the space behind, the air moving ahead) but also within us—intimate with our thoughts, and therefore with everything:

> "I know you despair at noon, when sky overflows
> with the present tense, and at night as you lie
> among those you have wronged; I know you have failed
> in what matters most, and use your groin to forget."

"What the Wing Says" is a Rorschach test we might wish all profound poems to deliver, so we could know them to be intimately our own and intimately others' at once. Like our lives, the poem is fueled by emotion, inconsistency, and constant questioning—and in these the poem finds its answers, and asks us to do the same. We must have an expansive outlook so as to allow many options, accept the natural and the instinctual, and trust the mysterious presences of beauty:

> "Does the future move in only one direction?
> Think how roots find their way, how hair spreads
> on the pillow, how watercolors give birth to light."

Nothing will be easy (" 'Think how dangerous I am' ") because nothing will be fixed, in our lives or in this poem. But everything–an everything we cannot pin down or encompass–will be available to us, offered up by this wing we might interpret, variously, as the natural force of the birds we have all longed to be; the supernatural flaming song of a god's angel (and even of the god itself); or the off-stage echoings of our own best selves, crying out to the spotlighted, day-to-day body we place before the world's audience.

* * *

Poem after poem limps across my desk, held up by the twin crutches of sensitive intelligence and passionate good intention. I say this not with malice, but with sadness and hard-headed respect; poems are seldom written by stupid or mean-spirited people, and this fact needs to be remembered by everyone–especially editors. Nonetheless, the writing of outstanding poems requires much more, demands those rare combinations and instances of imaginative rendering–one might also say "creative genius"–that are so impossible to describe or predict. Like a swarm of squirming puppies or snakes one is trying to keep inside an open-topped box, the best poem constantly gets away from us. It has more eyes and legs and tails than we do, to say nothing of quicker reflexes and better instincts. But we love it for its escaping as well as for its feel in our hands, so we give it all we've got–again and again.

The Carolina Quarterly

Founded 1948

A Cosmos in Words:
On Editing and Katherine E. Young's
"Nearing Chernobyl"

Christopher J. Windolph

The importance of small periodicals to writers and their audiences cannot be overstated. Their pages introduce literary talents, initiate current trends, developments, and tastes, and foster a literary life that nourishes. For over fifty years–an impressive lifespan for any small journal–*The Carolina Quarterly* has been housed and published in the English department at the University of North Carolina at Chapel Hill. Founded in 1948 as successor to the *University Magazine,* a forum of arts and letters launched in 1844, the journal publishes three issues per year, "quarterly" being a term derived from the old three-quarter academic calendar. We welcome submissions of all kinds and styles–fiction, poetry, belle-lettres, essays, interviews, and reviews, as well as photography and artwork. One thing that makes *The Carolina Quarterly* attractive to writers is that those without major publication credits are eligible for the yearly Charles B. Wood Award for Distinguished Writing, a $500 prize for the best poem or story published in each volume.

Editors play a vital role in the operation of small journals. Day to day, we oversee the influx of mail, work with staff readers, worry about the number of subscriptions, and pay the bills. Far more important, though, is how we direct the scope and mission of the periodicals we edit. As poetry editor of *The Carolina Quarterly*, I expect the poems printed in our pages to appear one day in chapbooks, collections, or anthologies, because the staff readers and I are confident that the poems we select deserve an audience. As well, they represent the best of what we read and comprise the range of our collective tastes and judgments.

Editors, however, are not just gatekeepers whose sole function is to exercise final approval over what will or will not appear in their periodicals. Let me illustrate by explaining the editorial process at *The Carolina Quarterly*. On average, we accept between one and three percent of unsolicited manuscripts. At least one member of our editorial board, which is typically a group of about ten members, closely reads all submissions. In deciding what to print, first we exclude poems that are clearly subpar. Those with promise are then sent on to a second reader for further evaluation, though the first reader may occasionally forward a submission exhibiting clear talent past the second reader altogether. If the second reading is favorable, a submission goes into our pool of "finalists" for consideration by the entire board. From these ten to fifteen candidates, a selection culled out of many hundreds, the editorial board makes its recommendations during periodic meetings. We read these poems aloud and vigorously debate their merits, working toward a consensus, if not a unanimity, of opinion. As the poetry editor, I oversee this process and make final decisions about what to print.

I most enjoy what I do because I encounter poems fresh from the writer's desk, long before they appear on the printed page. I imagine these words and phrases existing as a living impression in the writer's mind. The best poems result from an ongoing creative process, and although writers expend a great deal of effort before submitting their work, I recognize that their poems have yet to appear in public form. Assuming what I read may be unfinished, I try to answer this question first: has the poet completed what he or she wants to say? Many poems draw my attention, but finding a poem in which every single word is perfect beyond question is a rare, exceedingly delightful event.

Out of a group of ten finalists, the editorial board may recommend five poems for publication. Occasionally, I will add to or subtract from this list. I will then write to every finalist, explaining to those who do not make the cut why their poems received serious consideration but were not accepted. To those writers who are not accepted, I explain what we find appealing in their work and sometimes make suggestions for slight revision. Quite simply, an editor ought to be one who points out what does and does not work. Overall, this correspondence proves to be rewarding, both for me and for the writers whose work I find engaging, as most writers greatly appreciate feedback from an editor. Of course, time does not allow me to comment on every submission that comes into my hands, and often I never learn how my suggestions are received. But writers whose work I return write back frequently to say that their poems will incorporate the revisions I suggest when they appear in print elsewhere. What greater reward there can be for an editor, I do not know.

The editorial process described above is long-established policy. Because graduate students edit *The Carolina Quarterly*, editorial positions revolve every year or two. Remarkably, this aspect of the journal's operations has little effect on its mission, the quality of work appearing in its pages, or the regularity with which it is published. In fact, revolving editorship proves to be one of *The Carolina Quarterly*'s strengths, ensuring that we continue to value a variety of works—from the innovative to the traditional, from the local to the worldly. This characteristic is one I believe our readers most appreciate.

* * *

The Carolina Quarterly has a dual mission: to present the best works both by writers with established reputations and by those at the very beginning of their careers. We consider all genres and styles because we uphold the belief that no single approach can contain the art of poetry. Thus, we do not seek to promote any specific movement, ideology, or aesthetic. We seek *writers,* writers whose work deserves an audience of appreciative critical readers.

By saying writers "at the very beginning of their careers," I mean those writers who have no established reputation but who we think one day will. The author whose poem appears below, Katherine E. Young, is an example. Young's work first appeared in our Fall/Winter 1998 issue and has subsequently appeared in our Fall/Winter 1999 issue. She lives in the United States now, but for many years she lived and traveled extensively in Russia and the former Soviet Union, working as a diplomat, journalist, and businesswoman. Her coverage of Russia during the first Chechen war appeared in *Russian Life.* As you can see from the poem that follows, her experiences overseas have had a vital impact on her writing. While you read "Nearing Chernobyl," notice how it invites us into its world.

Nearing Chernobyl

Ukraine, 1987
Nuclear fallout is odorless, colorless, invisible to the naked eye.

Outside a village we stop by the road:
the air hangs pale, the gold-leaved birches
shiver dew from their fingers;
the crust of the earth breaks beneath my feet
as I pick a path in the tentative way
that cityfolk walk upon unmown grass.
But there's tentative and tentative—
and this morning I examine every blade, every stalk;
jump at each crackle of the shifting frost;
fear that enchantment will steal over me.
As if enchantment can be smelled on the wind,
or tasted in a gooseberry. As if
enchantment rides on the backs of the farmers
busy plowing the fields there,

beyond the trees; or rises, steaming,
from this tree root where I have crouched,
concealed. Perhaps I shouldn't touch
the tree's bole, the long grass;
perhaps then it will pass me by
as in a fairy tale whose heroine
wears an invisible ring to wander
unscathed through Death's portal and back.
For there's enchantment aplenty here:
the cold wheeling of comets; the breath
of the radiant sun howling down
on the pale rump of a woman peeing
in a Ukrainian forest. I carry the dust
of the universe on my shoes.

Perhaps the first thing one should notice about this poem is
its form: six sentences in twenty-seven lines, averaging about five
lines per sentence. The marked exception is the last one, a short
declarative of ten words—clearly the focal point. The poem's task
is to make these words—"I carry the dust / of the universe on my
shoes"—meaningful, to make them vivid and alive with suggestive
power. I mentioned above that this poem invites us into its world.
It does so by providing increasingly focused circles of intimacy:
in the Ukraine, by a road outside a village, at morning, sur-
rounded by fields, crouching near the base of a tree, close to the
earth and touching the grass. By the end of the poem we are
caught up in the immediacy of the here and now, and the furtive
relish of a private act. Present-tense verbs and gerunds help us
along that path. But far more important is the deliberate pacing
of the poem and its careful narrowing in focus to a single, simple,
defining moment of human existence. Who among us has not
been in these woods and sought this momentary, private release?

At the same time, we see corresponding and increasingly ra-
diating circles of feeling and thought. Notice the appeals to our
senses—especially touch—in the first six lines. The gold-leaved
birches shivering dew from their fingers are especially powerful.
Notice, too, that in the remaining lines the circles expand from

tactile images to varied realms of perception. We move from feel-
ing tentative, examining with curiosity, and jumping with appre-
hension to fearing a full surrender of self to the scene. We are then
invited to embrace wider orbits—of pastoralism, of enchantments
and fairy tales, of wheeling comets and the howling breath of the
sun, and finally of the dust of the universe—all in the context of
journeying down a road. The cosmic vision of the poem, quite
Whitmanesque in its design, collapses these oscillating spheres by
abruptly drawing us back to the immediacy of the moment: dust
"on my shoes." Our gaze is not directed upward into the sidereal
abyss, but downward toward the earth, back to the private apo-
gee of self-emanation and back to what we see over the tops of
our knees while crouching among trees. You would be right to
recall that Whitman was a poet of the grass, of the open road, and
of the recirculating self. "I bequeath myself to the dirt to grow
from the grass I love," he says. "Look for me under your boot-
soles."

Recall, too, that Whitman claims, "every atom belonging to
me as good belongs to you." Here, such transidentification comes
at our own peril, and this is where Young reformulates the
Whitmanesque vision in original, contemporary terms. We re-
member at the poem's end, almost with surprise, that this dust,
this "enchantment" covering our shoes, is in fact nuclear fallout—
an odorless, colorless, invisible poison that makes our intimate
contact with the earth of this place quite dangerous. We emerge
from an ecstatic rapture only to come face to face with human
mortality and frailty. We are confronted with the tension between
a desire for intimate knowledge of the world—in the tasting of a
gooseberry, or the splitting of an atom—and our own disruption
of that venture. This is not to say the Whitmanesque vision of all-
inclusiveness is inoperative here, as the qualities I point out col-
lectively demonstrate the liminality of this time and place. Not
knowing how this tension will be resolved, or if it even will, is a
major source of this poem's emotional power.

"Nearing Chernobyl" is a poem I will always remember from
my tenure at *The Carolina Quarterly*. It represents, in a nutshell, the
qualities our editors look for in a poem. Focused without being

narrow, personal without being cloying, original without being quixotic, it connects itself to a wider poetic heritage and endeavors to push beyond. Anchored in what we already know to be true, it invites us to see, feel, and think in ways not yet tried. It is as modest as it is grand. Our editors look forward to more like it in the future, and we welcome all submissions. Owing our success to the loyal readers, contributors, and benefactors gained through over five decades of publication, we say to these and to all, many thanks and good reading.

The Beloit Poetry Journal

Founded 1950

Experience Through Language:
On Philip Booth's "Seventy"

Marion K. Stocking

Picking a representative poem is a bit of a challenge for a magazine that has published Charles Bukowski and Philip Larkin in the same issue (in 1957, at the beginnings of their diverse careers). *The Beloit Poetry Journal*'s editors have aimed since our founding in 1950 to select the best poems we receive, regardless of form, school, style, length, subject, or reputation of the poet. One satisfaction is that we have been first or early publishers not only of Bukowski and Larkin, but of–among many others–Galway Kinnell, Anne Sexton, Philip Levine, A. R. Ammons, Sharon Olds, James Dickey, Maxine Kumin, Hayden Carruth, Gwendolyn Brooks, Robert Creeley, and recently Sherman Alexie.

Decisions are always made by an editorial board of plus or minus seven readers. At present, fewer than half are in academic life. Our backgrounds and predilections vary widely, and each has an equal voice as we attempt to reach consensus. The procedure is this: I do the initial screening of what currently averages out to thirty-eight poems a day. (That's nearly 14,000 per year.) Most go back within a week. Having done this for nearly half a century, I have a pretty good idea of which batches have a chance of acceptance; these get a cover slip with a date and my comment. When all the editors have commented on all the circulated manuscripts and I have returned those that are clearly not going to make it, we meet at a quarterly house party to read aloud all the survivors (usually about thirty batches) without naming the poets, and to discuss them until we come to decisions. We talk about accuracy of information, accuracy of image; we argue about ontological and political stance; we consult dictionary and encyclopedia; we let our individual passions show. We work for understanding of each others' responses to every poem.

A decision may be instantaneous, with a cheer, or may take hours. Some are painful; we frequently end by rejecting poems by friends, by loyal contributors, by poets with formidable reputations. Most of the poets we accept are people we've never heard of. We go on the assumption that some among them, just like Kinnell and Brooks and Alexie, will go on to be major powers in our literature. And then we clear the decks, and I write the acceptance letters and contracts.

* * *

What then would a representative poem be like (disregarding for the moment the long poems, which have historically been among our strengths)? It would have the stamina to survive diverse critical readings. Carelessly worded, self-indulgent, single-dimensional, and merely descriptive poems drop out early, as do many that are flawlessly workshopped but fail to ignite. The rare poems with fresh and distinctive language, or with a comic spirit, or that broaden our cultural perspective–these get special attention. Those that make it through tend to achieve an imaginative transformation–to move us in some way to a new place, to change or enlarge the way we comprehend the world. Above all (with the obvious exception of a concrete poem) they make a memorable music when we read them aloud. This act of passing each poem vocally through the body of the reader has been one of the most valuable of our selection processes.

I am now choosing, from the great diversity of poems we have published, one of exquisite music and with transformative power. It happens to be a poem by one of our earliest discoveries–Philip

Booth, whom we first published in 1952. But this is a recent poem that not only exemplifies qualities we editors profoundly appreciate but also moves me more deeply each time I read it. As Denise Levertov used to say of a poem she loved, "it nourishes me."

Seventy

Zero out the kitchen
window. Up 2° from
noon. *Too cold for snow*

we used to say. The radio
says flurries. Our bones
know better now, our noses

smell the metal sky.
By three, a big low
off the coast; we know

its January weight.
Power lines down. Whorls
of horizontal snow.

At iron dusk, the white-out.
No other house in sight.
Drifted beyond compass,

we light two candles, bank
the woodstove, move up stairs.
In this barely anchored bed

we let our legs warm up
our feet. Which mingled, heat
the rest of us against

the deep old dark. All night
the constant roar: as we once
dove from rocks to swim, we

let old waves wash over us,
waves like this storm,
fetched from a far shore.

One needs to read it aloud to feel the dance of the phonemes with one's breath and vocal cords and tongue and teeth and lips. The *o*'s and *oo*'s and *ou*'s establish and control the first section. "Whorls / of horizontal snow" becomes almost onomatopoetic, confirmed later on by *roar* and *storm*—words that act out in sound and throat the force they describe. In the middle, the *a*'s of *candles* and *bank* and *anchored* indicate a change from observation to action. I find only one word—significantly, *flurries*—that is not part of some weave of sound.

At a narrative level the movement of this poem is linear, but its structure is more complex. Formally it is not strictly metrical; the form follows the function, varying as the content moves. Its effect is to throw maximum impact on each word, using as few unstressed syllables as the language will allow, thereby forcing the reader to proceed very deliberately. The impact of the short lines is to move the reader thoughtfully from perception to unfolding perception. Even an enjambed line balances us for a half breath before we learn where it is leading; as the enjambments and the punctuation compel us to put a weight on each word, we feel the heft of it before we realize the concept.

Listen to the tonal and rhythmic shifts in these three lines:

By three, a big low
off the coast; we know

its January weight.

The short lines allow a delicate syncopation between lineation and syntax. And each line has its own music. The division into tercets further paces the poem, slowing us down and inviting small surprises as the syntax loops over. And that syncopation, especially in the opening lines, with their brief bulletins from the front, is enhanced by the small silences of the sharp caesuras. Although we can read these as three-stress lines, I sense only five light syllables in thirteen words, with rhyme and position throwing a special weight on *know*. Any other lineation would weaken the emphases and destroy the cadences.

The larger architecture of "Seventy" is four tightly integrated but distinct sections. The first, through "the metal sky," with its choppy syntax, orients us and then establishes and resolves the tension between the radio's *flurries* and the bones' knowledge. The second brings on the weight of the isolation, as predominantly end-stopped lines inform of what "we know." The wonderful line "Drifted beyond compass" which bridges the second and third sections establishes the inner action of the poem and carries us on into the "deep old dark." The possibly generic *we* of "we used to say" becomes the explicitly intimate *we* who light the candles. Finally, "all night" extends the action inward and outward, in time and space, to its resolution in one long, sinuous sentence.

In addition "Seventy" has a dialectic force: cold/heat, summer/ winter, silence/roar, light/dark, ignorance/experience, intimacy/ distance, climbing/diving, threat/security, outer/inner action, sensuous detail/infinite continuum.

A Philip Booth poem always rewards attention to the poet's handling of time and space. The title here provides one time frame: seventy is three score and ten. The narrative time line is simple: continuous present—afternoon to night in four stages—but casting back into a lifetime. The space begins external—"kitchen," "off the coast" and "move up stairs"—but enters an interior space with "Drifted beyond compass," in which all meanings of *compass* wonderfully apply. "Seventy" ends with this synchronicity:

old waves wash over us,
waves like this storm,
fetched from a far shore.

Thus time and space form a continuum on three levels: the literal impact of the present storm, the memory of literally swimming (here the vehicle of a metaphor), and the ambiguous "far shore"—both the literal origin of the storm and the vehicle of a metaphor with an inexpressible tenor.

Booth's language is colloquial and crisp, but each word means all the things it has meant and can mean. *Rest* works doubly. As the language moves into metaphor, it acquires powerful resonances. "Metal sky" and "iron dusk" are weighty tropes. "Drifted beyond compass" introduces a sailor's language, with the drifting snow giving way to the mental drifting beyond all bourn in the "barely anchored bed."

The poem could have ended with the three lines:

our feet. Which mingled, heat
the rest of us against
the deep old dark.

Heat, emphasized by punctuation and lineation, suggests more than warmth—a mutual heat that is a stay against not just the present cold but "the deep old dark" as well. That wonderfully resonant phrase, with its vowels moving back from teeth to throat, might have made a memorable closure. But what the poem is really about does not fully emerge until the final lines, so compressed and original as to (quite properly) defy paraphrase.

It is only when we have reached that "far shore" that we can sense the full range of energies that give this poem its power. One is the energy of a complete mutuality. No *I*'s here—only *we* and *our*. "Seventy" is a poem of shared consciousness raised, as I read it, to a level of heat that implies the power of the relationship against oblivion. It is, among other things, a love poem. It is also a portrayal of a consciousness, acutely sensuous and observant, attuned to the natural world and in harmony with it. It is further a poem about a balance between the discipline of volition ("we let," "we let," and that strong verb "fetched") and the drifting of the unconscious "beyond compass" into the oceanic. By the arts of the poet-musician, Philip Booth has in "Seventy" carried the reader from "zero" to a profound relationship—with a partner, with the natural world, with the half-submerged psyche, and with the age the title commemorates. One of our editors put it this way: the poem drifts him "beyond what I can fully comprehend." Another said it moves her through language "to a place irreducible to language."

I heard a story recently about a panel of poets and critics, with Helen Vendler, Marjorie Perloff, and one of the Language poets (Charles Bernstein?) on one side and Gerald Stern, Louis Simpson, and the late Denise Levertov on the other. Someone was insisting that "poetry is just language," to which Levertov beautifully replied, "No, it's experience through language." It is just such "experience through language" that "Seventy" gives the reader.

Given the diversity of work we have published, no one poem can represent all of "what we are looking for." But speaking for myself, I respond to those qualities that distinguish Philip Booth's work: the purity of the language, the accuracy of observation, the mastery in the music, the scope of the imagination, the way such a vision enlarges the way I comprehend the world. The possibility of discovering such poets and such poems makes opening those dozen or so envelopes every day an adventure, even after half a century.

Shenandoah

Founded 1950

The Light Through the Trees

R. T. Smith

Walking along a runnelled hill on Reid Road near my home in Lexington, Virginia, I was fascinated by the variety of barriers and obstacles the early autumn light has to evade to reach the gravel. The forest on either side offers great oak trunks and slender dogwoods, limbs, vines, a host of leaves, the feathers of resident crows, and the myriad needles of pines, all filtering out the light. A poetry editor's thicket of inclinations is likely to rival the intricacy of any forest. And yet, believing I play an active role in shaping my aesthetic forest, I keep reading, weighing, considering (*com* + *sideris*, with the stars), and ruminating over the many hundreds of manuscripts sent to *Shenandoah*. Because I trust that other editors are operating on the basis of their own careful subjectivities, I am confident that, acting separately, we create a wide and effective net for discovering and publishing skillful poetry.

It is easy enough to describe the mechanical process surrounding the sifting and selecting of work for *Shenandoah*. The common parlance would begin by saying that the poems have been "submitted" to us, but that word has always seemed inappropriate. The reason lies in the adversarial implications of the etymology (*sub* + *mittere*, to place under). I prefer to think that poems are placed under our care and that my role is one of stewardship. To assure effective custody of the manuscripts, I have tried to keep the logistics simple: upon arrival, poems are logged into the computer on a program ironically called "Paradox," and then I read the work and decide whether or not it's a possibility for *Shenandoah*. Those poems that do not appeal to me enough to receive further attention are logged out and sent back in their SASEs by interns, while any poems which strongly interest me go into a wire basket in my office under the photograph of a wintry oak. As the time to shape another issue approaches, I go through the poems slowly, choosing, arguing with myself, making notes, hoping this is one of my most clear-headed times. Poems which get this far into my consciousness will be accepted or regretfully declined with a note. Because the editor of a quarterly must value prudence and dispatch almost as much as taste, I strive to make all this happen in six to eight weeks. Because I read all the poems myself, I don't always succeed.

George Garrett has said that an editor's primary job is to say no, simply because it's any editor's most frequent decision, the most prominent feature in the daily log. I have to say no to about 4,000 prose pieces and close to 15,000 poems every year, but the highlight of my routine is the opportunity to say, "Yes, hell yes, yes absolutely." In my five years at *Shenandoah* I've been able to accept about 400 poems, partly because I've expanded the magazine by forty pages per issue with a prejudice toward the poetry section.

Now, trying to select one poem from that sheaf of acceptances in order to reveal here the texture of my editorial thought and taste, the barriers and passageways in my own thicket, is a daunting task. Among those 400 poems, there is no chaff to blow away. Recent poems by Carolyn Kizer, Mary Oliver, Lisa Williams, and Donald Platt were especially difficult to eliminate, but I eventually decided to present Brendan Galvin's poem "May Day," from our Spring 1997 issue, because it's a wonderful poem residing right at the heart of my enterprise as an editor. It has a formal feel without being rigid or predictable, it employs an intricate rhetoric that keeps getting richer with repeated readings, it offers a rich provenance because it speaks to and from an important tradition in the poetry of the English-speaking world, yet its imagery and reference are distinctly American. While I believe all the poems I select for *Shenandoah* have a pleasing shape and texture, like a warm stone lifted from the forest floor, the very best, like "May Day," seem to be geodes. When opened, they bend and alter and fulfill the light in unexpected ways.

May Day

Suddenly tugged from behind, the work
of an oriole, one spray of the apple tree's
floweration is trembling, looking the way
it feels when a fish begins nibbling
on your line. Isolations of nuthatch
and chickadee are slowly giving way, warming
into affinities. It began a month ago:
goldfinches blew into the pussy willows
and swung on the stems until we saw
that the uppermost catkins
had already sprung their bee fuzz.
Think of Catesby sketching a tree frog
clinging to the New World's
skunk cabbage, or his buffalo of the woods
engaging an itch with a bristly
locust tree: those juxtapositions,
like you and me, that prove it takes
two of anything to make something happen.

This is not a fashionable poem, not cryptic nor elliptical, not shaped by rant, riffs, surreal wit, nor explicit politics. Its more obvious strategies are orthodox (aware of but not subservient to a set of conventions), and Galvin, having heard both the arguments for rigorous form and those in favor of extravagant freedom, has opted for the role of an attentive and inventive fence walker, as the verse here is neither "new formal" nor unruly. "May Day" acknowledges rhetorical conventions that antedate our current notion of "creative writing" by several hundred years, but what I love about the poem is that its creativity is quiet—an iota here, an increment there, a touch-by-touch subverting of the predictable, confirming Dickinson's assertion that "The Truth must dazzle gradually." I believe this happens because the poet's goal is not to announce some stance or vision, but to discover the texture of intellectual and emotional experience by allowing things and actions their accurate names. While poems that feature a display, whether actual or imagined, of the writer's personal life seek to bring everything into the light, and hermetic poems strive to order the shadows, Galvin engages the interplay between light and shadow, which has always been the territory of the primary, even primal, theme of "May Day": it is a love poem.

"May Day" also courts that often misapplied label "nature poem," for it displays nature in informed detail and suggests a belief in the unquestionable value of precise observation and naming. It is also a nature poem in the larger, more crucial sense, in that it concerns "whatever is begotten, born, and dies." To underscore the connections between the cycle of the seasons, flora and fauna, and the frisson of human love, Galvin sets his poem right after the sweet showers of April on a date that not only signals spring renaissance but also is associated with the celebration—not always genteel or euphemistic—of mating. And all along he is quietly troping, introducing the beloved listener into the poem very quietly as the impersonal "your" of line five gives way to the understood "you" before line 12, which becomes explicit in the "you and me" of the penultimate line exclaiming the subtle gestures of birds and trees on the first day of May. Widening his scope to a natural history of friction and juxtaposition, the narrator adjusts his attention to praise the intricate dance that results in sustained love, and he reels the reader in with the sensitivity of an angler.

"How did it happen," asks CzeslawMilosz, "that to be a poet in the 20th century means to receive training in every kind of pessimism, sarcasm, bitterness, doubt?" Many of the poets who send to *Shenandoah* work infused with joy and optimism, that old "passionate intensity," seem to lack craft; in contrast, the polished and honed work is often tinged with a promotion of personal experience that seems to well up from a cynical source and lacks conviction. "May Day," in contrast, offers an intricate texture that urges no oversimplification; it is built of a careful, alert rhetoric whose components interlock in that nearly invisible way that we mean to praise when we say that language "flows."

Even a glance at "May Day" will reveal that it operates in the three arenas I find necessary for a poem to satisfy my readerly needs. The vivid images (mostly visual) in the poem–the trembling blossoms, the "bristly locust tree"–engage the reader on a physiological level, bringing the body into the act of reading the poem beyond an obvious involvement in the sounding of the words. This occurs partly because the observation is vigorous without being insistent or strident. The emotional or affective apparatus activates more slowly, but the "trembling," "nibbling," "clinging," and "engaging" are all terms with amatory dimensions providing the thread of an argument, what the poet is, as he admits at the end, out to "prove." The nature of that argument supplies the center of intellectual gravity: by what process *does* "something happen"? Through implication, insinuation, a gradual gathering of momentum, and this is the testimony of "May Day." Invoking Catesby's paintings as witness to the same sense of magnetic necessity allows Galvin to supplement his intimate description of interplay between two people with a historical dimension.

This is only a part of what I mean by saying that good poems are like geodes. I knew when I first read this poem that its method of sustaining the central metaphor did not signal caution or dispassion, but a rich ambivalence. The phrase "May Day" signifies not only the pagan celebration of dull roots stirring with spring rain, but also the maritime code for distress, and the possession by Eros has long been recognizable as distress. So any misplaced suspicion of the "merely pleasant" is dispelled, and the reader is invited to listen harder. Such an invitation always raises a poem's value for me.

"May Day" also rewards other areas of interrogation. Its camouflaged resemblance to a sonnet, its botanical façade, its transition from the general "anything" to the specific but understated "something," its application of sweet reason to the natural world:

these all contribute to the poet's participation with earned author-ity in the centuries-old conversation we know as the sonnet tra-dition.

Although I have no editorial prejudice against long poems, I still see economy as swift discourse working within the confines of the necessary. Some long poems are wonderfully efficient, some short ones are windy and wasteful. An economical poem like "May Day" is marked by its invitation to the reader to read its silences as well as its cadences, by its continuing to reward excavation.

All these considerations may begin to suggest a forest around my road so dense that hardly any light could filter through at all, but the great corrective, the most likely intrusion on any theory of what makes a poem valuable, is the sound. The internal echo-ing of important words in a poem—what Brooks and Warren in *Understanding Poetry* called "the tangled glitter of syllables"—coop-erates with rhythm to create the poem's unparaphrasable atmo-sphere. Here's a single line: ". . . it feels when a fish begins nib-bling." The alliterative f (on stressed syllables both times to ensure the impression of deliberateness), the internal rhyme ("when" / "begins") and the assonant short is all find echoes in the preced-ing and following lines. This strategy, pervasive in the poem, pro-vides a quiet intensification beyond the usual music of speech. This richness is reinforced by the sounds the sentences make be-cause, even in the space of such a short poem, Galvin has relied on a varied and sinuous but absolutely clear syntax to ensure that his four sentences achieve and sustain traction. As much as I ap-preciate an accomplished villanelle or sestina, I think the center of *Shenandoah*'s poetic project rests with poems which, like this one, lack the rigid governance of a fixed form but observe a care-ful decorum which provides a trellis to support the original and organic.

Perhaps my choice of "May Day" will demonstrate that the role subject matter plays in my selection of poems is negligible. I'm not, as a rule, drawn to love poems, even when they, like "May Day," open a Pandora's box of questions. (Are the lovers equally active, for instance, or must one be more passive?) Neither am I intrinsically hospitable to subjects such as diet plans, fiber optics, or Jimmy Stewart, yet recent issues of *Shenandoah* feature poems about these subjects. The poems that I love and want to publish engage me with a strangeness that is neither accidental nor gratuitous. They aim to delight and instruct, rather than immersing me in an "experimental" outburst of cagey fragmentation. They establish their own decorum, then subvert own protocols for discernible purposes. They are radiantly skillful and refuse to accept the stored gestures of English as a finished language cooling on the mortuary slab. They satisfy no objective system of criteria, but what I hope is an informed, sensitive, and generous subjectivity.

I am surprised but not dismayed that all this actually sounds a little conservative, though less, I hope, in the sense of political conservatism than in the sense of environmental conservation, as I retain the urge to conserve the metaphorical liveliness, meticulous invention, and ambitious inquisitiveness that drew me to poetry and to the vocation of editing to begin with. Although *Shenandoah*'s offices are in the Southern highlands, our ambitions are international, transcultural, omnivorous, always eager to discover the next surprising excellence. I believe our current readers know this already, and I hope that those who aspire to see their work in our pages will look closely enough at our contents to see for themselves.

Even the most carefully constructed language has a tendency to unravel, and what I seek for *Shenandoah* are poems whose unraveling is intriguing and moving. This can only occur when the poems have been woven with craft and emotional investment evident in aural echoes, tonal continuity, connotative overlap, a kind of tesserae effect whereby the parts of the poem, speaking to the audience, also speak to each other and become one song. The question of whether or not I can love particular poems, then, will substantially involve the ability and willingness of the poet to preside over his or her language, no matter how raw and hot the materials come, to shape them leaf by leaf, sound by sound, because I want *Shenandoah* to display all the variety and harmony of a thriving natural habitat.

The Northwest Review

Founded 1957

On Failure

John Witte

This much is certain. The evidence piles up every day on editors' desks. More Americans than ever before are attracted to the blank page to write and share their most intimate feelings with strangers. They seem undeterred by the rejection and frustration that poets are likely to face. A deep yearning is felt in many of these poems, a sense perhaps of the inadequacy of our material forms— our architecture and landscapes, houses and automobiles, our commodities—to express who we are. Perhaps poetry stands in dialectical opposition to television, and the suffusion of media throughout our culture has triggered a poetic counter-action . . . a longing for pure utterance.

Promising to fan these first sparks of inspiration, creative writing programs have proliferated, growing from ugly ducklings to the swans of many graduate English programs—and certainly their golden geese. Literary journals have sprung up at an even more dramatic rate, thousands of issues appearing at regular intervals, each filled with the earnest stories and poems of a nation's restless scribblers. Never have so many been drawn to the well. But are we writing better? Are we reading better and more closely?

The editors of literary reviews are the recipients of much of this writing. Often a young writer has no other serious reader with whom to share his or her work and receive an honest evaluation. Every author must know that this is a responsibility gravely assumed. First (after the paraphernalia of envelope and cover letter and SASE is set aside), we read each submission thoughtfully and generously. Any work showing a glimmer of promise is shared with another editor for a second, perhaps different reading. When a work is to be rejected, we do so respectfully, including, when warranted, a heartening note. At the next level of consideration, the editorial staff gathers to critique, discuss, read aloud, and make final decisions on the poems that have generated the most heat. From the five thousand poems submitted during a given four-month acceptance period we select eight or ten (rarely more) for each issue of *Northwest Review.*

Personal predilections–call them taste–can never be completely excluded from the editorial process. We can be wrong, even spectacularly wrong. Virginia Woolf, to pick but one famous example, declared Joyce's *Ulysses* the literary equivalent of adolescent scab-picking. An editor working alone is sure to blunder by and by. Accordingly, at *Northwest Review* we have enlarged the process, convening a group of experienced senior editors of equal rank who must reach consensus to publish any poem. We have represented among our half-dozen poetry editors a wide spectrum of backgrounds and literary inclinations, narrowing the odds that we'll miss something, and providing for every work, whether narrative, feminist, formal, or imagist, an informed and insightful reading. We create in this way a finer net, and cast it further. And consensus–by which we mean that each editor finds the work worthy of publication (not that he or she personally adores it)– protects against any one opinion dominating the magazine. Our hope is that *Northwest Review* will welcome any and all styles and perspectives, continuing to be (as Carolyn Kizer once described it) "eclectic but not promiscuous."

In his essay "The Age of Criticism" Randall Jarrell slyly observed that, "around the throne of God, where all the angels read perfectly, there are no critics–there is no need for them." But here on earth, given our fallibility as readers, how are we to identify what is truly original and enduring–work that will, by definition, almost certainly strike us as unfamiliar, even discomfiting? This is the test of an editor: how honestly and open-heartedly, and with how vigorous an imagination and how keen a hunger, has he or she engaged the poem under consideration?

Every poem is judged on its own terms, and on its own merits. Consensus may emerge quickly, or it may be achieved gradually, over an hour or two of sometimes fractious deliberations. The following quotations, from poems appearing in recent issues of *Northwest Review*, illustrate the variety of work we publish, as well as the different avenues each followed to acceptance.

In "Harem Scarem" by Susanne Kort we were immediately struck by the scrimshaw detail of the imagery, and its "blue desire," but only after we began to feel the emotional undercurrent did we agree to publish it. Here are the opening stanzas:

> It has all been born, I think, or most of it,
> from an acute wish for order: a blue desire, to give it
> color–
>
> if you could have seen
> her bedroom, or the sideboard
> in our dining room: piled up
> with Stradivarius débris, her chaotic
>
> linoleum, the stairwell where the phone was
> on top of the books & galoshes, on the way
> to her erratic bureau,
> her air tarnished mirrors & combs,
> the rings she'd leave off, in mysterious formations,
> to weigh down the letters my Daddy wrote
>
> to all of us: his faraway harem . . .

By contrast, we were at first put off by the dense verbiage, the twisting linguistic labyrinth of the following, from the sonnet sequence *Critical Opalescence and the Blueness of the Sky* by John de Stefano. The poem seemed designed to exclude the reader:

The terminal had been left idling, lit
dully up, an off-shade of parched orange,
the system sloppily malapropped, chunking
along, hawking morsels of the impro-

cessable. It was a feast-fast or binge-
and-purge economy. You were the riddle—
the superfine sieve, or metapunc-

tilious discriminant—and the sponge,
blackly-soaking-it-all-in. . .

But a lively discussion of the poem began to reveal its originality
and ferocious lyricism, its gorgeous diction like clotted honey. A
hard-won consensus was achieved to see this poem into print.

With so much of modern poetry tethered to one wound or
another, David Kirby came to us like balm: we loved the brio,
the brassy irreverence and goof-ball hilarity of "The Big Jacket,"
which begins:

The French soldiers are stooping and circling
    each other with their hands behind their backs
à la Groucho Marx—it's La Scala, and the opera
    is Donizetti's *La fille du Règiment*, but the set
is, first, an Alpine range like something you'd see

in an Ed Wood movie, with painted-on goats
    and mountains that threaten to topple over whenever
a careless peasant bumps into one. . .

Reading a poem aloud, trying it against the tongue, is a regu-
lar and important part of our consideration process. The sound
of the following poem, its intricate alliteration and glottal stops,
along with the urgency of its message, won us over. In "Butter,"
Kyoko Uchida explores how language exposes us as "outsiders"
(the mother), and "insiders" (the daughter), then gradually re-
verses these roles:

My mother couldn't make the sound of two t's, the quick
flutter of tongue against palate, hard stop: muttering
but-ter, buller, budder after me at ten, she drove me to
utter despair . . .

. . . So I cluttered my own daughter-tongue, scattered them
sharp as slow pitter-patter of water on rotting woodwork,
dull as the clatter of steak knives flashing against a
fine-patterned cloth . . .

. . . It had made my mother sick at school those
Occupation years, rich yellow squares of fat she wasn't
allowed to waste. It ran strong as hunger inside her
raw mouth, oiling the small working parts, loosening
the fettered tongue to say its animal smell
aloud. But it wouldn't fit, clotting thick in her throat,
and all of this going down rancid, bitter.

A poem like "Butter" invites readers to enter, gradually in-
forming and involving them. Others, like "A Harvest" by Mark
Levine, drag the reader under. We were frustrated and provoked
as editors, unable at first even to locate the poem in time and
place, yet almost knocked down by the authority and muscular-
ity of this voice. I quote this poem in its entirety:

A Harvest

The ponies arrived: we were poised for absolutes.
Then a word—*arrows*; and a stiff-legged climb
to the toolshed of our elders, our betters;
there to minister endangered fluids

that still had the power to enchant.
Turning and turning our blades through living soil.

Pioneers we were. Often we found
a mule in the desert and offered it desert burial;
toiling to defeat the unclean grasses; to restore
to the landscape a missing color, like a scratch.

For the burial in the desert of the Hebrews is a fact.
And the burial of the pretenders, and of their songs.

Panic ascended and fled. One: the glad sight of a tree
bent towards the city with ribbons of illness
wound in its bark and in its inner layers.
Two: the harvest of eggs. Two: the harvest of perfection.

We sent for the girls for an evening of paternity and dance.
Mine had a big bellyache. The opaque waters turned

symbolic in evening's rust. I crawled beneath
my swayback mare and confided my misgivings.
Alone in the new snow with my clamp and my
pollution and an apprehension of love's chemicals.

Every decade a war song. Sometimes I feel like a *(what?)*
a child swaddled in eternal fabrics.

The glad sight of a tree grieving.
The glad sight of voices raised to the fatherless sky.
A train arrives from the city, seeking comfort
for its squawking cargo, and we turn the train away.

The writing seems reckless, incongruous details caroming off
one another and the walls of the poem. A black humor flickers
over the lines, the images often absurd or surreal. The mood shifts
abruptly, wrenchingly, from tragic to light-hearted. And the vari-
ous pasts of the poem—the pioneer West, the European Holocaust,
the Biblical exodus—multiply and increase the reader's unease.
There is a continual refraction of image, the "toolshed" releasing

or morphing into a magician's apothecary, and the burial of the dead mule becoming a "burial in the desert of the Hebrews." Like a nightmare into which we wander and find ourselves trapped, the poem jolts dizzily forward, proceeding by indirection, distraction, detour.

The Biblical desert of Egypt and the desert of the American West are overlaid like a palimpsest. And the diction of the Bible, the "unclean grasses" and "the burial of the pretenders, and of their songs," converges with the aw-shucks cowboy lingo of "a big bellyache," and "my swayback mare," causing an exquisite dissonance. Or is it an unfamiliar harmony?

As the various fragmented narratives accumulate, of the Holocaust and the American genocide of the Indian people, there emerges a monstrous picture, a chimera. Applying the logic of exploitation, the poet projects the destruction of the Indians to the devastation of the land for the material of manufacture, "turning our blades through living soil," reaping a strange "harvest," with its attendant "pollution." The poem beginning "poised for absolutes" ends, as we have just ended this bloodiest of centuries, with a crisis of faith, our "voices raised to the fatherless sky." We sense that the poem has prepared, but not delivered, an indictment, one that will name the poet as well as the reader.

From its confidently declarative opening lines, through its kaleidoscopically shifting arrangements of imagery conflating and manipulating histories, to its unnervingly ambivalent ending, this poem is difficult, dazzling, cranky, demanding, and richly rewarding. We enthusiastically agreed to publish it in *Northwest Review,* along with a clutch of Mark Levine's other poems.

* * *

None of these poets has yet established a wide reputation, though two have first books. They pursue a variety of professions: one is a psychiatrist, another a translator, a teacher, a journalist. For most of them, this represents one of their first appearances in print (though hardly their last). Our purpose at *Northwest Review* is not to locate timeless poems, worthy of inclusion in anyone's canon.

It might even be said that we have accepted these poems because they took too many chances, getting too far out on the risky limb of imagination, failing in extraordinary, unforgettable, and beguiling ways. We invite the reader to question with us our presumptions about literary success. The poems discussed here grope in the dark, as all real art must, leading us forward. They succeed by failing, as Beckett said, and "failing better."

Chelsea

Founded 1958

When the Search Succeeds

Richard Foerster

Objectivity–the editor's first responsibility–I find is the most difficult to uphold. It is all too easy, for me at least, to be biased from the outset, either for or against a poem, by such things as the writer's fame or obscurity, a publishing record outlined in a cover letter, or even the condition of the paper the work is typed on. I am also aware that everywhere in the daily give-and-take of human interchange is the tendency toward nepotism–the natural desire to help friends or those in a position to return a favor. It is an ever-present danger for an editor, especially for one like me who is also a writer. I try to set a course to avoid these clashing rocks and, like an argonaut, to keep my mind on the quest.

However, there can be no editing without subjective decisions. An editor brings the whole baggage of his being to a poem under consideration. Every editor is an amalgam of prior influences: family upbringing, education, political and religious affiliations or lack thereof–everything that has nurtured him as an opinionated being willing to subscribe to a particular set of ideals. All these influences, but especially the poets and critics I studied in school and afterwards on my own, have left me with a panoply of predispositions, of likes and dislikes regarding a poem's subject, sound, form, purpose, and total effect. And yet I suspect my taste in poetry depends less on an acquired understanding of poetics than it does on an intuitive aesthetic sense—a natural ability to appreciate, for example, both parterre and wayside gardens, Monteverdi and Mahler, Mantegna and Turner, and areas between and beyond. Be open, I tell myself, to the new, but also to the old in new guises. Literary editing, then, is at best a balance between disinterested judgment and an indulgence of personal tastes.

So, picture me on a Sunday afternoon in the spring at the public library in Katonah, New York, listening to Jane Flanders read her work. At the time, I had seen only individual poems of hers in literary magazines, but must have been sufficiently impressed to want to sit and hear more. Among the new poems she read that day was this one:

The House That Fear Built: Warsaw, 1943

*The purpose of poetry is to remind us
how difficult it is to remain just one person,
for our house is open, there are no keys in the doors . . .*
        —Czeslaw Milosz from "Ars Poetica"

I am the boy with his hands raised over his head
in Warsaw.

I am the soldier whose rifle is trained
on the boy with his hands raised over his head
in Warsaw.

I am the woman with lowered gaze
who fears the soldier whose rifle is trained
on the boy with his hands raised over his head
in Warsaw.

I am the man in the overcoat
who loves the woman with lowered gaze

who fears the soldier whose rifle is trained
on the boy with his hands raised over his head
in Warsaw.

I am the stranger who photographs
the man in the overcoat
who loves the woman with lowered gaze
who fears the soldier whose rifle is trained
on the boy with his hands raised over his head
in Warsaw.

The crowd, of which I am each part, moves on
beneath my window, for I am the crone too
who shakes her sheets
over every street in the world
muttering
What's this? What's this?

I remember enjoying initially the sound of this poem, the way
it evoked not only "The House That Jack Built," an eighteenth-
century nursery rhyme that some scholars believe is based on a
sixteenth-century Hebrew chant, but also Elizabeth Bishop's "Vis-
its to St. Elizabeths." The incremental repetition of such poems
has its roots in medieval ballads, in the plainspeak and melodies
of communal entertainment, and I found myself responding to
this ancient aural technique and the haunting mood it generated
in counterpoint to the poem's World War II setting.

I was moved also by the poem's other sound effects, though
I can't say I was conscious of them on first hearing. The labels
come with hindsight. Now I detect an almost Anglo-Saxon use of
alliteration and caesura to enhance the syntactic balance of many
of the lines, such as:

who loves the woman with lowered gaze
who fears the soldier   whose rifle is trained

Assonance and approximate rhymes thread through the stanzas, stitching together images and ideas:

stranger gaze trained raised
and
beneath sheets streets

"The sound must seem an echo to the sense" is one Popean truism I find ignored by too many poets today. Flanders makes her sounds serve sense in a striking way. Like Eliot before her in "The Hollow Men" ("This is the way the world ends") and—to my mind—like Ravel in "La Valse," she uses traditional rhythms to overthrow tradition, to give us a glimpse of the deterioration of order. Against the ironic counterpoint of the innocent children's rhyme, Flanders unfolds a widening perspective of the horrors of twentieth-century war. Her rhythms and incremental repetitions undermine our initial expectations. The skipping rhythm introduced in the first stanza leads us to believe that the boy's arms might be raised in play. By the poem's end, however, we realize he is part of a gruesome, complex tableau of the Warsaw Ghetto Uprising of the spring of 1943.

Like the crone muttering *"What's this? What's this?"* I wanted to see this poem after I had heard it, and so at the end of her reading on that Sunday afternoon, I asked Jane Flanders to submit it to me at *Chelsea* for consideration by the entire staff. I was delighted when it arrived a few weeks later.

Reading it confirmed my initial aural impressions: child's dance becomes *danse macabre*—like the simple, playful march tune in the first movement of Shostakovich's great *Leningrad Symphony*, which rolls along, gradually crescendoing into a juggernaut of martial terror. The progression of the poem's images and ideas seemed to me both surprising and inevitable; appropriately for a poem based on a photograph, they moved cinematically, from close-up to panorama, from boy to crowd to "every street in the world."

Seeing the typescript also made clear for me the relationship between the epigraph and both the title and the subject of the poem. "Our house" I understood not only as Parnassus and the poet's ability to assume masks but also as the entire modern world, which seems increasingly invaded and controlled by fear. The poet / spectator of this drama is helpless to prevent herself from identifying with each of her characters. Unable "to remain just one person" as Milosz says, the poet becomes a part of each of them, shares in their fears, love, brutality, and indifference, and imparts these to us through craft. Reading the poem, I too found myself becoming each of the characters: boy / victim, soldier / victimizer, resigned woman, compassionate but equally helpless man, one of the crowd that "moves on," and finally the onlooking crone, who in traditional nursery rhymes shakes out the world's woes from her bedding. In Flanders' modern version, however, the crone cannot absolve herself of complicity by pretending not to understand the nature of the tragedy occurring beneath her window.

I also enjoyed the double-edged words that add to the poem's depth: *Warsaw* became in my mind "war saw"; the soldier's rifle is not aimed but *trained*, suggesting the political indoctrination that made young German men into instruments of the Nazi Reich, tools of the Final Solution; and finally there is the crone and her sheets: I imagine her not only attending to her domestic chores but also hiding behind the sheets of a newspaper, the way we overlook the world from our armchairs while muttering "What's this?" when certain headlines catch our eyes. Consider: if we change "Warsaw" to "Kosovo" and the date from 1943 to 1999, the universality of Flanders' horrific vision becomes even more fully apparent. In the time since those earlier atrocities, the human race still has not cleansed its house of ethnic discord, and we as readers, as citizens of the world, share in the blame for letting fear win.

Ultimately, the totality of Flanders' poem—a serious message conveyed by alluring yet haunting means—made me recommend it to my colleagues for publication in *Chelsea*. We subsequently nominated "The House That Fear Built: Warsaw, 1943" for a

Pushcart Prize, which it won, and so another set of editors must have responded to the poem in much the same way that I did. The greatest satisfaction I have as a literary editor—and I suspect I speak for many of us—comes from sharing such personal enthusiasms with others through the printed page of the magazine. And I am grateful to have the opportunity to recommend this poem again.

The Laurel Review

Founded 1960

Pilgrim's Progress: A Sequel

Wherein Mr. Editor Struggles Against Assorted Foes,
Including Himself, to Discover his Destination
and True Reward

William Trowbridge

It's 11 a.m. Saturday. I could use a day off, but the sidewalks need shoveling, we're out of bread and coffee, and I have fifty freshman themes and thirty-five essay tests to grade. However, since breakfast I've been reading from the large stack of manuscripts I've brought home in hopes of helping keep *The Laurel Review*'s editorial promise of a four-month maximum response time. It was harder to keep when the three co-editors' teaching loads were twelve semester hours. Now each of us has a three-hour load reduction to help produce two issues per year of the magazine and a poetry chapbook for the GreenTower Press chapbook series–a job that takes more time than teaching a three-hour class.

Like most middle-sized literary magazines, *TLR* gets thousands of submissions, publishing less than one percent of them. As I turn to the next manuscript, which I notice has been with us for five months, I'm becoming conscious of two familiar editorial syndromes. One is the Fog, which drifts into my mind when I've been reading for a couple of hours straight, especially when I was tired to begin with. I find it harder to perceive details, subtleties; I start mentally squinting–as Poe said you have to do when reading a poem longer than one hundred or so lines. Pushed beyond that limit, he insisted, the mind tires and the rest of the poem becomes merely "a series of brief poetical effects"–partial visibility due to Fog. He was being stingy about the number of lines, but he certainly had a point.

The other syndrome I call the Gotcha: reading a manuscript with the primary purpose of finding a reason to reject as early as possible, thereby making that large stack of material on your desk shrink faster. I don't think this was what *Kenyon Review* founder John Crowe Ransom was talking about when he said he published every manuscript he finished reading. The Gotcha syndrome, like the Fog, results from fatigue, and it turns the editor into the writer's adversary. So, till the Fog drifts off and the Gotcha troll crawls back under its bridge, I need to shovel the walks or go get the groceries. Come to think of it, I could use a year off, and I wouldn't be too choosy where.

And why am I whining about all this to you, who also has a life that's no stroll through the Tate Gallery? It's just to let you know the conditions under which your manuscript might be read–especially if you're submitting to places that don't have full-time staffs (i.e., most literary magazines). I'm not even so sure the conditions are better at big operations, which, though they usually have full-time editors, get lots more submissions. So how do you give your work the best chance to shine through the Fog and dodge the Gotcha? I don't think the answer is "hooks," or look-Ma-no-hands phrasing, or high-profile trendiness. And it's certainly not the cute, chummy cover letter. Then what? I'm glad I don't have to be with you physically when I say this: you just need to write really good stuff.

"Very funny," you say. "And what, exactly, is your idea of 'really good stuff'?" Now you've got me–and with what's probably the question most readers of this book want answered. And you're probably tired of hearing that there's no specific formula or list of qualities anyone can offer you, though that's true.

Maybe I should just say that I know what I like and back rapidly out of this little essay. However, I sometimes end up choosing a work that shows me I don't know what I like. And maybe

that leads to a good rule for an editor: don't know what you like—
so you won't blind yourself to what's outside your comfy little
neighborhood. Don't know what you don't like, either—because
that kind of knowing can make you just as blind. I'm not endors-
ing the know-nothing school of criticism. I just mean an editor
shouldn't marry a set of notions about what makes good or bad
literature. Or perhaps, like those members of other monastic or-
ders, an editor just shouldn't marry. I think an observation of
Randall Jarrell's serves best here. The ideal critic, he said, "has
not set up rigid standards to which a true work of art must con-
form, but . . . has tried instead to let the many true works of art—
his experience of them—set up the general expectations to which
his criticism of art conforms." Surely this applies to editors as well.
Let me try to give you an example of what I mean by most of
the above.

Some time ago, as I was squinting through the Fog and try-
ing to juke the Gotcha troll, I came across a poem by Allen
Braden. Here it is:

Crew Cut

The barber says he never did love her
without ever using that word.
Behind a stripe screwing up the pole as if by magic,
his scissors lisp *bitch bitch bitch*.
My father and the other married men—
some for the second or third time—
nod and pocket their fists.
The clipper strips my eight-year-old skull
until it's stubbled as a new beard.
Over the *grrrs* of the razor
he tells them—no—tells *us* the lies
she bewitched the court with,
the demands she put on him.

Once his work is done
I bristle like a man's supposed to,
step down and take my father's seat.
Snapping his sheet for us
like a magician's cape,
our man releases my curls.
He's ready to close up
and perform his story
for happy hour next door.
Father pays up. He'll go home,
even though the chores are done.
He'll take me back to his wife
and try hard to say the right things.

A read-through told me this was the kind of poem I didn't like, that the very subject, a boy's first "official" haircut as an initiation into traditional manhood, was shopworn, perhaps appropriate to a list of ideas to help unblock undergraduate writers. And the Fog made the poem's plain language and ironic tone seem to offer a commonplace treatment of that commonplace subject. On first reading (which is all most poems submitted to editors ever get), "Crew Cut" seemed too much like the other hundred thousand accessible, realistic, narrative, competently written poems that travel back and forth through the mails. "Gotcha," croaked the troll; "Zzzz," went the Fog. "And besides," nagged their cousin Mr. Sleeps-with-Marketing, popping a breath mint, "we need more NAMES in this issue." My hand began slouching toward the rejection slips.

But something in the fourth line held me back. The barber's scissors "lisp *bitch, bitch, bitch*." What word choice! How surprising and how absolutely right. Scissors speak with a lisp. And what do these scissors have to say about the subject at hand? Well, you heard 'em: bitch, that scissors word, that sound that is "an echo to the sense"–not only of the word but, in this case, of what proved to be the lesson the barber is offering about women. Mr. Pope and Mr. Perrine would sing their approval, cheek to cheek.

The Fog began to clear, though the Gotcha muttered something about a monkey and a typewriter.

Rereading, I noticed another wonder, this one in the second verse paragraph: "Snapping his sheet for us / like a magician's cape, / our man releases my curls." Braden's boy has been changed as if by magic, his pliant, effeminate curls "released" by the magician, whose clippers have stripped the "eight-year-old skull / until it's stubbled as a new beard." Something magical has happened in, of all places, a barbershop. And the magician simile, like the word choice in line four, is both surprising and exactly right, as are the beard/curls contrast and the ominous image of the skull, suggestive of the darkness—the death both of innocence and of "softness"—beneath the surface of this happy public occasion. I was reminded of my favorite John Crowe Ransom word, from "Janet Waking": the boy has been *transmogrified*, changed into a different and somewhat grotesque form.

Thus far, this "series of brief poetical effects" I'd experienced after the thousand or so lines of poetry I'd read that morning was compelling enough to dispatch the Fog and the Gotcha and persuade me to read "Crew Cut" a couple of more times. I was at full alert, and the writer had me where every writer wants to get an editor: hoping the rereads will live up to the really good stuff that flashed out during or, as in this case, after the first time through. I wasn't disappointed.

"Crew Cut," it turns out, is an intensely ironic comment on a traditional kind of gender indoctrination (and I really don't like gender poems). Barbershops (vs. "styling salons") are male-only establishments. The very term *crew cut* derives from the way oarsmen cropped their hair in formerly all-male rowing competitions. This boy is being made—transmogrified into—a member of the crew. However, despite the temporary power of the barber/magician/misogynist over the young initiate, this ceremony doesn't succeed; the magic fails to have a lasting effect. Though the boy takes his father's chair in the circle of the initiated, he at least suspects that the father, still his main male role model, is not a fully participating member. And the ironic view of the initiation further suggests that the son, whatever the father felt, has afterwards developed his own point of view, perhaps at odds with his father's and certainly with that of the culture "our man" the barber represents.

The ambiguity of the closure keeps this poem from dropping either into Walton Family snuggliness, in which Dad demonstrates the theme that a man can be made of nobler stuff than is seen in the boys at the barber shop, or into a trendy bit of adult male bashing in which he doesn't. The boy's father ignores "happy hour," where the other men are headed, and takes his son home, where the father will "try hard to say the right things." Does that mean he will reveal he doesn't accept the crew's view of women or that he will merely assume a pose while at home? Though the shift from present to future tense in the final four lines implies retrospect, hindsight, the son can't really know the father's true feelings. And so, Braden chooses the rich ambiguity of authentic experience over the strip mall of the easy and expected.

The first thing that caught my attention about this poem was the language, that scissors talk. What I came to like most about the poem's language was what I at first didn't like: its simplicity, its plainness, which is appropriate to the poem's speaker and occasion—and which, during my initial, Foggy reading, disguised its subtlety and musicality. Allen Braden creates a rough music. For example, note the "heavy" *d* and *b* consonance, the low-vowel assonance of *u* and *a,* and the rough accentual texture in the line "eight-year-old skull / until it's stubbled as a new beard." The poem's vocabulary is spare, and the predominantly short lines and sentences create a tight-lipped, just-the-facts-ma'am terseness, the very way a "man" is trained to speak. Though the poem's not written in traditional meter, a scansion (often helpful when analyzing so-called free verse) reveals a frequent use of spondees (in thirteen out of the twenty-four lines), which gives a kind of tom-tom emphasis to key phases like "try hard" and "right things." There's even a double spondee in "lisp *bitch bitch bitch."* Tom-tom beats, a gathering of males focused on their masculinity—nudge, nudge; wink, wink; say no more.

But wait a minute: what happened to all that stuff about not knowing what I like and don't like? Can't my critical bias be inferred from what I've said I liked about this poem? "Another moss-backed formalist critic," you may think, "probably with no appreciation for work that doesn't lend itself to that closed, linear, meaning-obsessed, close-reading, 'academic' mindset." Well, maybe, but I think I was just meeting the poem on its own terms.

I didn't know I was going to like this poem at all. I almost knew I *wasn't* going to like it. But some of the really good stuff in "Crew Cut" caught my attention, which caused me to notice its wealth of really good stuff–only some of which I've discussed here. I was also happy to have discovered a publishable work by another newcomer. Such discoveries, I think, are one of the most important functions of a literary magazine.

The North American Review

Founded 1964

Staying Amazed

Peter Cooley

That for thirty years I have been poetry editor of a national maga-
zine still amazes me. Like most editors probably, I did not grow
up around literary magazines. They weren't present in the school
library of my Episcopal high school in suburban Detroit, or in the
local public library I frequented, and there were only a few in the
tiny Midwestern liberal arts college I graduated from. At eighteen,
on my first trip alone to New York City, I discovered to my de-
light "literary bookstores" and came upon the likes of *Partisan
Review, The Hudson Review, The Beloit Poetry Journal,* and *The North
American Review,* all of which I purchased and took home to read
and try to understand. I know I liked their colorful artistic cov-
ers and the peculiar ads in them for other magazines and for
books I'd never heard of. Eight years later, by serendipity, I pub-
lished my first poem in *The North American Review,* and four years
after that, by another serendipitous twist, became its poetry edi-
tor.

Today, though bombarded by print as teacher and editor, I
don't take this job for granted. Like other editors, I have my mo-
ments in which American writing, I am convinced, is in decline
like our whole civilization, due to the ease of printing on the com-
puter, the Internet, whoever is President of the U.S. or governor
of my state at the time. But taking a long glance backward, po-

etry seems as healthy now as it did in 1970 when I took on the job. At *NAR* we currently publish more women writers than before, but this is due to the phenomenal renaissance of women in the arts; we publish too few poems from a recognizable minority perspective because we, alas, receive too few. And we do not solicit.

Yes, most of the submissions which come in are silly, amateurish, boring. Why not? Their writing problems are attributable to insufficient reading of poetry (often the submission is some kind of prose in drag), insufficient craft, insufficient or confusing feeling. These are all the problems one encounters in teaching Introduction to Creative Writing. Anyone reading this article who writes can find those insufficiencies in himself or herself at some point in time.

Usually a new bundle of poems (and we receive about twelve thousand a year, all of which I read myself, though for spacing reasons I can accept only around fifty) is enough to fill me with hope that one envelope will have that "Je ne sais quoi" which allows it to leap out of the slush pile and amaze me enough for a second reading. Amaze me enough for a third. Amaze me enough to accept one of the poems. Certainly, after thirty years, I can glance at the poems and see if they will arrest my attention. Title, first line, arrangement of lines, last line: experienced glancing has taught me how to find the poems we may want. I have little new to add to what most of us believe a good poem to be. Reader, you know: a new insight on experience, freshness of language, depth of feeling, wit perhaps, control of line and music, music, music— the element most free versers are neglecting nowadays. When I took this position a friend suggested that, given the long-standing history and reputation of the *NAR,* a certain kind of poem was what we were looking for. I think not. Pound's "Make it new" is enough for me. I just don't see the new often enough.

Instead, writing the cover letter appears the major creative act for a poet. Yes, life is tough: we know that. But to hear of the author's abusive parent, recovery through therapy, botched career, tedious job, demanding children, broken dishwasher or car or toilet, dying parent, dead kitten, impotent husband, rat-infested barn, or frigid wife is not to claim my attention. We all have our problems. Even less compelling is a list of credits, particularly if some of them are fabrications I can unravel by checking the latest issue of another magazine. Farther down the list is some claim to admiration of my own work or a reminder that the author and I have met at a party I never attended. At the bottom is an invitation to spend a romantic weekend at the poet's apartment in New York or San Francisco or Key West. These invitations have come from both men and women.

Floyd Skloot's "Visiting Hour" has those qualities that demand my attention at first glance and keep it fixed for continuous re-readings. I must admit I opened his envelope knowing I might be interested in the contents since I had seen his work elsewhere and liked it. Yes, forty years later, I am still reading the literary magazines, now with access to a university library where I have ordered most of the subscriptions. Naturally, I subscribe to half a dozen such magazines myself. Here is the poem:

Visiting Hour

We came straight from school
crossing the island as winds
rose and fell. From half
a mile away the whitecapped
baywater smelled of fuel oil,
marsh grass and autumn
darkness. Gulls circled
a trawler nudging the dock.
We gathered in an alley
behind the old hospital
where our fathers recovered,
or declined, or lingered
behind the cold panes keeping
them from us. We were too young
and full of dangerous life
to be allowed inside. Stroke,

cancer of the lung, a broken
hip, severed arm, failing heart.
We named our fathers by what held
them there. Clot, stone, spine.
Taking turns to stand on one
another's shoulders, we tapped
on windows as the sun set.
Fathers smiled within the folds
of their faces, waved, lay back
among the pillows. They turned
white before our eyes, became
empty spaces in our lives,
quiet behind glass in their
gleaming ground floor rooms.

Skloot's first line attracted me since it propelled the narrative.
I knew, too, the narrative would be lyric in intention from glanc-
ing at its structure. I was attracted to the first-person-plural
speaker, tired as I am of confessional "I" poems. Line two intro-
duced a situation which intrigued me and possessed almost he-
roic overtones. The first of a number of triumvirates appears in
"fuel oil, / marsh grass and autumn / darkness," threesomes al-
ways surprising in their combinations. The offhandedness with
which the speakers describe the father's conditions, "recovered,
/ or declined, or lingered" fascinated me as did the "Clot, stone,
spine" by which they name the fathers.

The group process and group identification as the children
stand on one another's shoulders, and the steady enjambments
which have parceled out the emotional information, kept me in
suspense. Finally, we are allowed glimpses of the fathers seen col-
lectively. What is most astonishing about the poem is what it does
not say: that "I" is contained in the "we"—that *I*'s father is present
among the "Fathers [who] smiled, within the folds / of their faces,
waved, lay back / among the pillows." I find the last four lines
graphic and horrifying, especially since I must draw my own
emotional conclusion as to the speakers' feelings.

The pull between catalogue and lyric narrative, the iambic

tetrameter line modulated from its base in "We named our fathers by what held" to the trochaic tetrameter of the last line: these are all part of the inner beauty of "Visiting Hour." Unpretentious, unprepossessing, it works its way upon us with sonic and rhythmic claims yet leaves us to draw our own conclusions.

The young man from Detroit on his first visit to New York would have read this poem several times through, especially if no one were watching. He stands here, in the narrow aisles of the dusty bookstore, frightened by the sophistication of the bored female cashier, in black turtleneck and smoking a black cigarette, he has passed on his way in.. He will buy the magazine, delving into his small cache of spending money. I edit for that young man, who only knows that he loves poetry and tries to write it (badly, of course). I edit for him because he still waits inside me for the next bulging envelope I tear open with my pocketknife. For the next time, unprepared, he is amazed.

Hiram Poetry Review

Founded 1966

Indulging Our Whims

Hale Chatfield

It was an ironic attitude I brought to the founding of the *Hiram Poetry Review* in 1966: I was sick of reading through poetry magazines and being disappointed with the poems I found there. I supposed that the superabundance of dull poetry was due to a superabundance of poetry magazines—all competing for the rare item of truly good poetry. So what's ironic? I decided to try to compensate for all that overkill by producing still *another* poetry magazine. The idea was this: *HPR* would publish only those poems which actually *wowed* one of us editors. We would reject good poems that were less than absolutely compelling to at least one of us (usually the one or two who are actually doing the work on a particular issue). We would reject mere competence along with clear incompetence. We would take only those poems which were delightful to read. What's more, we wouldn't worry much about *why* they were delightful to read.

I don't know how uniformly we delight our readers, but our acceptance policy hasn't changed. We take as many or as few poems in six months (we publish semi-annually) as manage to really please us.

Rawdon Tomlinson made a minor mistake about five years ago when he sent us "Fat People at the Amusement Park." We accepted the poem (I'm really crazy about craziness), but Tomlinson's address appeared only on his SASE. So when we sent him our acceptance letter, we sent it in an envelope bearing the only record we had of the poet's address. When we realized what had happened, we put the poem on the back burner, hoping we'd hear from its author some day so we could do all of our usual paperwork and get the thing into print. I was really disappointed that we couldn't use this poem right away.

Fat People at the Amusement Park

They are laughing like the rest of us,
amused at being here
among bright lights and whirling things

laughing, despite their particular knowledge
of gravity, which is why they ride
the fastest and highest rides,

a release from the demands of earth
between bouts with blue cotton candy,
stuffed bears and peanuts–

we watch them bounce along the midway
with their rosy-cheeked smiles and jouncing
asses, chattering as though they'd entered

the kingdom, they step into the cars
of the tilt-a-whirl, tilting, and take off
into a scream of weightlessness.

Good poetry, whether it is serious or comic, seems to me "a release from the demands of earth," and good poetry is sensitive to the language. There is for me almost a carnival pleasure in such a recognition as the fact that anyone who is able to laugh does so "despite" his or her "particular knowledge of gravity." The implicit pun on *grave* reminds us that life is essentially grave for us poor human beings, with our particular handicaps (our "fat-nesses")–and (perhaps Tomlinson also meant this) with death, the grave, always out there waiting to darken our moods forever. I *liked* Tomlinson's fat people, escaping unself-consciously into their robust joy, and it was sad news that we had indefinitely to post-pone the publication of this fine poem.

Happily, however, we heard from Tomlinson in a year or so. He wanted to know where his promised contributor's copies had gone. We wrote him at once, carefully preserved his address, and printed his poem in the next issue, along with another one, "A Good Night's Sleep."

So there's a moral to this story. Two morals, if you will: (1) if you're a poet, make sure your address is *on* your manuscripts, and (2) if you're an editor, make sure you have everything you need before you mail anything back with an acceptance.

I suspect that the chief message of this essay, though, is that there's precious little magic in our way of choosing poems for the *Hiram Poetry Review*. Sometime within two or three months of re-ceiving an envelope of poems one of us opens it and reads the poems. If that editor (these days it's usually I; sometimes Carol Donley) really likes a poem, it gets shown to another editor for confirmation, and two *yeses* confirm it. Sometimes one *yes* is enough, if it's an exceptionally hearty one.

It's worth noting that the delay of a couple of months isn't due entirely to our busyness or laziness (sometimes they're powerful, of course). The main reason for the delay is a conscientious, cen-tral commitment we've made with respect to choosing poems: we will not read them unless we're in an alert and receptive mood, and waiting for that mood in modern America sometimes is a long-term process. It seems to us wasteful and unfair to read people's poems the way we read ads and newsletters. We really want to read poems with the attention we'd like our own work to get, so we usually have to wait for the right moment to open a stack of submissions.

I can say a little about what I myself look for when I'm in a manuscript-reading mood. A couple of summers ago I was asked to prepare, for a writers' conference panel, a statement on the subject "What makes a good poem?" At first I was indignant, even angry. It seemed obvious to me that if I knew what "makes a good poem" I'd sit down then and there and make lots of them to advance my own fortune (!) and reputation. But I wanted to do a good job for the writers' conference people, so I decided to take the question at least half seriously. I'm glad I did. I searched my mind and came up with the checklist I've unconsciously used to select poems all these years, and now I use it to measure my *own* poems: (1) I want a poem to be *unique* (I want to know right away I've never seen another poem quite like it); (2) I want it to be *competent* (Wallace Stevens says we read poetry with our nerves; that's a real investment of ourselves—something like submitting to a lover. Incompetence in prosody, or even in diction, spelling, or punctuation, is painful to a poetry reader.); (3) I want it to be *concise* (I want to have the feeling that every word in the poem is necessary, that no word or phrase is there just for padding: when I encounter an adjective, I don't want to feel that it might have been omitted if its noun had been more carefully selected); perhaps above all (4) I want the poem to be *filled with adventure.* (At every point in the poem I want a sense of excitement about what must be coming next. If I try to guess what is coming next, I want to be proven wrong.)

I almost like it that Tomlinson's poem isn't what anybody would call a "great poem"; its delightful simplicity in a way underscores how able it is, for we enjoy it readily and easily. It neatly fulfills for me the four requirements listed above: (1) at no point do I feel I've read this poem before (even *now*, though I know the poem well); (2) surely it is competent, and even wise, as it helps us to understand how we are "amused at being here"; (3) in its fifteen lines it is restrained and economical (the poet resists any temptation to take us on a full tour of the park); and (4) even as I read it again and again, I'm tickled by the new goodies I encounter at every phrase or line, right up to the "scream of weightlessness" at the very end. I use this delightful poem in my classes often; I don't tire of it.

The Iowa Review

Founded 1970

Hearing Something
in the Syllables

David Hamilton

My response to new poems varies as conditioned by many things.
So any example I might summon here offers much less than a
rule. A reasonably pure example would be work from a poet com-
pletely unknown to us previously. Hence "Una Vecchia" by Zona
Teti, who "lives in Connecticut," according to her minimalist
contributor's note, and who, when we were considering her work,
was a name new to us.

First, though, I should stress how little inclined I am to stand
as a lonely arbiter and defender of taste. There are a few items in
each issue that I may include regardless of the opinions of oth-
ers. These choices may arise out of prior loyalties that I feel are
sufficiently earned; they may have to do with the history of our
magazine as I perceive it; they may record a personal view at the
time of what I consider an extraordinary story or poem, or they
may result from idiosyncrasies, even whimsies, to which I am
friendly. But these insistences are few. I can't think of an issue that
has contained many of them. Instead, in one issue after another,
we identify through discussion most of what we print.

Our staff is made up of graduate students, ranging in age from
their mid-twenties to mid-thirties. A few have topped forty. As

students, they may not have attained a "terminal degree," much less become full professors or senior partners somewhere or other which, in our professional culture, increasingly identifies the adult. But that is a ludicrous standard which we are glad to subvert. They are avid readers, write themselves, and have much to teach us—as they could teach others—about what they admire most.

I should add that we do not consider fiction or poetry from graduate students at Iowa, not while they are here. If it is a good story or poem, we say, it will be good a few years from now when you are somewhere else. In part we want to avoid having our staff feel compromised in workshops when they venture to praise a classmate's work. And in larger part, we simply believe it is better to put some distance between ourselves and the work we consider.

So you should imagine a small circle of readers, students who can come from any graduate program whatever, even law or medicine or physics. Some years, a colleague from the English department will have joined us. But the Writers' Workshop predominates, and a willingness to read regularly authorizes one's chance of making an opinion known and felt. Then this circle subdivides into groups concentrating on poetry or fiction. I join both. Our poetry group usually numbers five or six, and I suppose you could say that we try to take reading and readers about as seriously as we take writing and writers.

Together, we read and narrow the submissions. A few hundred unsolicited poems a week give us plenty of material for making selections, which emerge gradually from our reading individually day by day and from weekly discussion sessions. Often in those discussions a unified sense emerges from the group, with one person's observations reinforcing and extending another's. We love to find that happening and always assent to it. But we frequently give in to minority advocacy too, for we'd prefer a committed minority voice to lukewarm general assent. This is a magazine, after all, a transient and sometimes fugitive publication, a launching pad for art on its way somewhere else, and so a format that should be friendly to trial and error.

All the poems we print, save for the occasional piece that is simply my choice, have been read aloud in our meetings. Read aloud and discussed. Someone should be able to read the poem as if savoring it, and a few of us should be ready to talk about it with conviction.

Here then is the poem I mentioned earlier, a lyric by Zona Teti.

Una Vecchia

Leaves in the wind and a sea-wind smell
of salt and wet rot, loves of an old
woman when the boys go away
to the mist of girls.
So I too was mist
melting back into a mountain,
leaving at last clarity and stone.

But boys want to start to drown,
though most make sure they never finish,
asking mist to part to a sea,
asking death to stay a possibility.

Age is too far out to see.
Or rather the symbols of age.
The boys still go by codes
as if they knocked rhythmically
still on the clubhouse door.

And yet the boys are lovely and new.
You can't help thinking about them.
The new skin in mist. The oversized hands.
The new minds that die with a thought.

Usually what attracts me to a poem is its whisper of wisdom, a sense of thought and observation that I find fresh. Here, the second stanza delivers that jolt first, with its soft turn on "mist" now missing and leaving something harder. I find authority also in the expressed voice, real or imagined, of an older woman, a voice that would have to be effectively imagined even if it were "real," as we say loosely. In any case, I feel confident of Teti's understanding and find much wry truth in her meditations.

No denial of that freshness comes from finding that it plays off an old thought. Poems, after all, are "news that stays news"; in this case the news is Sappho's. Here is Mary Barnard's version:

Of course I love you

But if you love me,
marry a young woman!

I couldn't stand it
to live with a young
man, I being older.

It's as if Teti sought a more meditative lyric from a similar consciousness, and I for one relish the piggybacked effect, a "dialogical imagination" incorporating echoes of the anthologies that have made us. I love it even more when the brush of poem upon poem goes almost unnoticed, leaving my notice, or suspicion, an accident of browsing, more a proof of serendipity than of scholarship.

Teti's ideas and her sense of character attract me, but soon I notice the care she takes with sound–the rhyme of "sea" with "possibility," for example, playfully slant to the eye while to the ear it is exact. Next I notice the interlaced alliteration and assonance in the first line of the poem pulling me toward "wet" in the second, then the firmness of those monosyllables ending with *t* and their leading on to assonance again, but on a low vowel, *o,* before returning to the higher *i* and *ea* with which we began. I find faith in lyricism here, and a sense of the value of syllables– syllables before words, I suspect. As an utterance, the poem seems confident, alert to explorations, and understated.

Syllables before words? That's an odd thing to have caught myself saying. Sound before meaning, and meaning embedded in particles refracting in ways that may thwart or extend the writer's intentions. I don't mean to insist on this or to offer it as a rule for a fine poem. But I am intrigued and am almost always drawn in by the strange dance of syllables when modulations of sound coordinate them. I think I trust the experience and wisdom of the language over that of writers, and trust the writer more who submits him or herself to discovering discipline within it. That *salt, wet, rot,* and *mist* should share the same firm dental closure seems to me wonderful and to reinforce coherence, even harmony in their meaning. Then mist parts to a sea, and closure opens in both the sound of the syllable and in the idea.

Related to this integrity of sound is one of the poem's more risky tropes, its deployment of two puns: "So I too was mist" and "Age is too far out to see." These could be seen as outrageous, but I think neither is. In fact, my suspicion is that on first reading we fail to notice both and that the second, more obvious pun is there in part to help us notice the first. Perhaps it slipped past because enjambment and alliteration pulled us toward the next line, keeping "mist" a noun rather than hinting of a participle, and holding us to the peculiar thought of mist melting to stone. The second pun seems more flagrant, a cliché passed off as if fresh; that it comes second argues that it is no accident. Both are daring. Imagine the impulse to revise them out!

The second pun completes a triplet in rhyme—a faint reminder of those flaunted by Dryden and Pope—and that ups the ante. In fact there are two triplets in the poem—"mountain/stone/drown" and "sea/possibility/see." Stanza breaks interrupt both, quieting their effect.

These gestures seem to me soft echoes of the bravado of boys with new minds and oversized hands. The puns and extended rhyme hint at both immaturity and awkwardness. Teti's speaker can't help thinking about the boys, and in her sympathetic, even loving mimicry of them she risks self-betrayal. But mightn't she risk exactly that with boys who are "lovely and new," and mightn't Sappho have risked the same?

So these gestures, as I call them, which have the potential to be showy, turn out to be a form of understatement, emblems of restraint. The more expected posture would be for the speaker to tell more of the boys' seduction or hers, or her near-seduction, or self-seduction, and to milk it for proof of experience. But that is not this poem's manner, any more than seduction, really, is its subtext. The poem conveys instead some fading longing wryly held in check. A line and a half quite close to the end expose longing in all its rawness. "You can't help thinking about them." No, indeed you can't. Then the stab of jealousy, a visceral note of lament: "The new skin in mist." This not even fleshed out as a sentence, for a verb would overspecify. And I prefer it this way, with less certainty and with implications hovering as the final line and a half recreate some ironic distance. For what else dies with the thought?

This partial reading was not worked out in detail in our discussions. But it began there, and the poem has stuck with me, so I have gone back and developed our earlier thinking. As a way of making choices, this rather meditative reading is notable because it allows us to extend ourselves incrementally, our new steps leading from what we have known and valued. These extensions are full of variation and surprise, and in certain cases they may be a bit subversive, but our guiding spirit is hardly revolutionary. We are not seeking an entirely new track.

Were that to be so, I think we as editors would have to work more from principle than from poems as they are sent to us. I can imagine a decision to seek poetry of a certain kind, aggressively new and challenging in one respect or another, and a determination to define that challenge and to search for instances. Perhaps we would look for poems rooted in an ecological consciousness, or that undermine the grammatical assumptions of a sentence. However, deduction and the enforcement of principle are mostly foreign to our style.

It is probably healthy then that our staff changes from year to year. New readers introduce fresh commitments. The more variety we promote in the group, the more productively we destabilize the limits on ideas that our magazine is willing to entertain. Sometimes we are moved by work we do not think of as coming from familiar places.

No doubt, also, poems slip by us that could reward us as well as "Una Vecchia" rewards me. We try, but we have no way of guaranteeing each poem the reading it deserves. What then made this poem stand out one day and elicit an extended chance? Something heard, perhaps; call it the play of syllables. Our first reader may not even have heard it consciously. However that may have been, I'm glad we listened.

New Letters

Founded 1971

The Dynamics of Wit:
Choosing Poems for Publication

Robert Stewart

In choosing poetry for publication, an editor needs both discipline and freedom. A little craziness, in fact, keeps him from bottoming out on poems that fit a predisposition, whatever its kind. Poetry screening can easily become the most bureaucratic task at a magazine–paper shuffling to almost cartoon proportions. One envisions a mid-level clerk at his desk behind two-foot stacks of papers labeled "In/Out."

The process of choosing a poem for publication requires nothing more than the exercise of taste and judgment. The test of an editor is her openness to the eccentricities of each new poem; the test of each poem is to impress an editor who has just read reams of silly or otherwise lifeless verse.

It is to the latter category–lifeless verse–that I turn, briefly. In my twenty-odd years of evaluating poetry for *New Letters*, the competence level of submissions has risen steadily. Credit writing programs or the magazine's growing reputation. I'm not sure. Although this trend seems encouraging, it also represents a growing "middle class" of poems that have the trappings of culture and wit but not the sophistication. Given the volume of manuscripts submitted, an editor can actually welcome poems so obviously trite and amateurish that they can be dismissed at a glance. The other, larger category–the competent but dull–requires scrutiny.

A competent poem generally has visual imagery, with most

unnecessary adjectives and adverbs scraped away, and contains thematic and tonal consistency. It looks like the work of an accomplished writer but is really, to borrow a metaphor from S. I. Hayakawa, the literary equivalent of processed food—it looks and tastes like food but contains almost no nutritional value. Such a poem forces the editor to go back and ask why, if this is so well done, it does not move him. Why is it dull? After all, a dull poem by any standard is a failure.

The answer lies in the editor's little bit of craziness. When he reads in a poem about a young woman that "She's been rolled over / tongue studs for ages," as in "Tattoo" by Susan Whitmore, from a recent *New Letters*, will he be prepared for the bizarre logic of such an image? This is the kind of poem that easily could be missed, or avoided, except for its assumption of reversal, its perspective not anticipated. The woman has become minuscule, and the tongue stud large enough for her to be rolled over it. The image lifts our hopes; it supports our faith that something unstated elevates this poem beyond competence alone. Here, a woman actually becomes diminished by the intensity of emotion that centers on a tongue stud and magnifies it. An editor wants to find that kind of contradiction, or paradox, that kind of wit.

An unwitty poem starts at the rim of a canyon and ends there, still looking in, like a tourist holding to the handrail. An exciting poem starts at the rim of a canyon and sends us sailing, hardly feeling the leap, into the sky. The whole poem might be spent in midair, with the illusion of flight, of freedom, of the tenderness of the world. Even then, such romantic or sentimental notions of freedom, love, and goodness don't hold us for long. Something unsaid, perhaps overlooked, creates the tension, and the interest— that we are careening toward the rocks below.

John Keats asked, in a letter to his brother, "Do you not see how necessary a World of Pains and troubles is to school an intelligence and make it a soul?" In the context of his letter, Keats was trying to explain "negative capability," through which a poet comprehends both joy and pain in the same act. Whitmore's poem "Tattoo" makes this connection: "It is simple as a name needled into the skin, / Of those who can't let go what they hurt."

Craziness: We hold on to what hurts. The world of pains is more than a needle's prick; it is the memory of a past love etched into the skin. Wit is the way art acknowledges that coexistence of opposite feelings, keeping us a little off balance.

In selecting poems, one looks, finally, for ambiguities, for a recognition of uncertainties, or, in another kind of poem, for the discrepancy between what is expected and what is revealed. I want to look at an entire poem by Gregory K. Field from *New Letters*.

The Sea is the Longest Breath
   –to Crystal

The sea is the longest breath ever taken.
Its vast green chest rises again
before it can completely fall–
forever pumped by wind and moon.
This sailboat's engine is like
the biggest heart that ever beat,
its rhythm so strong the bulkheads hum.
Between this heart and that breath
a song drifts out over the sea.
It is the longest song ever sung.
It goes on for days,
passed on from hull to waves,
as we plunge and heave and roll
across the sea's nervous chest.
This song is for you.
Now you are the sea, the wind,
the moon and the song
that rises to sting my eyes,
coat my hair in salt.
Sing on past the time
the boat rests sluggish in its slip,
on softly to my years at night
when I am alone,

into my dreams where we both
stand on deck before I awaken
and you turn to me to say,
the sea is the longest breath ever taken.

The first thematic section of the poem, roughly its first half, ends with line fourteen, "across the sea's nervous chest." Through that first section, the images brim with connotations of life–almost pantheistic life–in words such as "breath," "wind," "pumped" and "hum." The rhythm is lyrical and fluid. We know, from the dedication, that the poem is for a woman; but is this a love poem or an elegy? While the skillful connections among the sea, the boat, and the living body imply the writer's competence, little so far suggests a "World of Pains," except the word "nervous" in line fourteen and, perhaps, the impressive power of the sea itself.

The first section engages us primarily in the way the imagery threatens to lapse into sentimental cliches about the sea but doesn't. Instead of the ethereal laziness of trite writing, familiar images of the sea lash against real knowledge–the wind as the "sailboat's engine," the power that makes the "bulkheads hum." This grounding combines with a consistent metaphor of the sea's "nervous chest" to suggest that the poet has his material under control.

Keats's negative capability emerges as we move deeper into the poem, in the second "section," which begins with line fifteen, "This song is for you." The unstated tension in the first half of the poem appears more directly in the lines,

Now you are the sea, the wind,
the moon and the song . . .

This *is* a love poem; it is also an elegy. The "chest that rises again / before it can completely fall" is not the heaving bosom of a lover but the deep breathing of life in distress. When Chinese philosophers said, "Inhale–Hallelujah–Exhale," they meant the human autobiography: inhale connotes life, exhale the end of life.

It is process itself that this poem wants to explore. Through death, the woman has become part of the natural world again, part of the sea. For the poet, the sea contains the ambivalence of love and loss. In the second part of the poem, we learn that the first part–the reassuring part–is a dream. Its seductive beauty contrasts with the central tenor of the poem–the wakeful time when "the boat rests sluggish in its slip." Further, this lifeless time–Keats's melancholy–contrasts in that line with the soothing alliteration of the *s* sounds, which shroud the emotion like mist.

The imagery and subject of Field's poem are reminiscent of David Ignatow's "Rescue the Dead," which equates love with death, a kind of drowning:

> To love is to be led away
> into a forest where the secret grave
> is dug, singing, praising darkness
> under the trees.

The tension of Ignatow's poem lies in its objective tone: To love is to die; to not love is to live. The same paradox arises in the Field poem: love, the source of joy, is also the source of pain.

Both Field and Ignatow accept life in its fullest terms, with all the risk that brings; and that risk is what they confront and celebrate. Ignatow ends his poem with ironic envy for those who do not love: "My boat wallows in the sea. / You who are free, / rescue the dead." Implied there: Ignatow's admission that he is one who wallows in the sea, one who loves.

These two poets, like others mentioned in this essay, illustrate that love and pain are at once opposed and linked. That's their wit. The tension of the Greg Field poem is in its restraint, holding back the message of loss so subtly it could be missed by a weary editor. Further, the lyrical beauty masks the suffering that is the poem's real engine.

Merely competent poems succeed in terms of style only. They do not recognize the ambivalence within a single event. Meanwhile, poetry editors face their haystack-high piles of manuscripts, looking for a glimmer of the unexpected before they lie down to sleep.

Obsidian III

Founded 1975

Mama Names Her God

Afaa Michael Weaver

Gerald Barrax and Duriel Harris are *Obsidian III*'s poetry editors. When I inherited the position as the third editor of the journal, one of my first missions was to build a system of communication. When I call Jerry, *Obsidian*'s previous editor, to discuss poetry, we begin or end by sharing notes on the western, Jerry's favorite film category. So a poet's opus may get sandwiched between our praises for *Shane*. Duriel is a poet as well as a student of postmodern funk, so her e-mails may contain phrasing that challenges my middle-age blind spots in the turbine of linguistic change. In all of this we work to seek and publish the new and the good, and we look for the occasional gem that glitters to signal a precious talent. We think all that we publish does indeed shine, but there is once in a while that poetic gift that brings light to the whole assembly. When this happens we celebrate. "The Two Marys" is the gem that signals the talent of Honorée Fanonne Jeffers:

The Two Marys

> Mary what you gone
> name that pretty little baby?
> —*Traditional Spiritual*

Alone here in our task—One woman
chained as saint, and another woman
misnamed as whore—now joined
as one mouth that shouts
the disorder of faith. Two pairs
of hands pulling threads from his robe.
Unbidden freedom from the spirit's
battering ram. Two pairs of hands
cupped under a womb, catching
thirty years of walking death,
of suckling from a gored
bosom. Phantom salt on our thighs
and our dream's neck snapped.
Mary. Nails break the water
of our keening. We wait for
his return as shrieking dust.
How can we justify the third
morning, his blood as wine?
No rolled back stone can dam this grief.
What you gone name that pretty little baby?
What you gone call your gospel?
Man prayer bread.

The "two Marys" offer one song, one resolve against the pa-
triarchal shutting down of women's voices, in this instance by a
religiosity that invites itself to interrupt what I choose to call the
Mary Spirit, spinning it into the madonna/whore binary opposi-
tion. The Marys act as one from their oppressed space, a margin-
ality ". . . as one mouth that shouts the disorder of faith." Using
the New Testament definition of faith, the Mary Spirit troubles
accepted notions of faith as ". . . the substance of things hoped for,
the evidence of things not seen" (Hebrews 11:1). In appropriat-
ing the power of marginality, the two Marys gather their forces
against a male ontology that has positioned itself against them in
hegemonic arrogance. In the transcendent vision that is part and
parcel of the vatic act of self-invention, the two voices in the Mary

Spirit speak: "[We are] alone here in our task." This is a solitary space they inhabit, because self-invention is anathema to the dominant presence, to the "God" of patriarchal deliverance to us of sacred texts.

Jeffers' poem came through the regular *Obsidian III* editorial process. Using our routing system, Mitzi Nuckols, the editorial assistant in our Raleigh, North Carolina office, mailed photocopies of the manuscripts to Barrax and Harris. They decided which of the batch to accept. I can imagine his decision-making taking place in the stream of his critical observations on a scene from *Once Upon a Time in the West;* I can imagine her weighing the merits of the poem in the context of meditations on Janet Jackson's Tina Turner as a missing text for the future. The editorial process suggests such conjuring of personal knowledge and poetics.

In "The Two Marys" poem, Duriel and Jerry have chosen a poem that takes its own meditations to dimensions of the metaphysical. The reflexive act is a gospel of spirituals, the annunciation of a repressed monotheism—the power of women to heal a tender bifurcation and name "God" with names they choose.

Jeffers begins by outlining the oppressed space as ". . .One woman / chained as saint, and another woman / misnamed as whore. . ." The poem proceeds along an ideational progression that is at once prayer and song—the rooted critique and courage of spirituals more than the celebratory and abiding gesture of gospel. With this bravery, the Mary Spirit perceives the divine phallocentrism as intrusive and, consequently, is moved to intervene in one eloquent subversion of prophecy, "Two pairs / of hands pulling threads from his robe." The robe is the tale whose original thread is spun in Old Testament prophecies, and it is the complex joining of the lives of these two Marys in the Mary Spirit. In the line's literal sense it is the cloth upon the life of the child, Jesus Christ, the Messiah.

The driving pulse in the lines of the poem is an irregular but steady percussive iambic, a thrusting that challenges the intrusion of the divine phallocentrism, "Unbidden freedom from the spirit's / battering ram." The two Marys protest this rod of fate that spins them out of an ordinary serenity to make them suffer the insufferable weight of bearing and losing children, and of being judged as invoking as saints and whores either too much or too little esteem. Jeffers' ironic pointillism manifests in the "unbidden freedom" to suggest the latent liberation inherent in being the subjects of divine exploitation. The devaluing of women is antecedent to the lives of these two in the Mary spirit, the historical phenomenon of immaculate conception, and their own burden of Christ's life, opens the gate for this subject/object positioning, this liberation launched in the liminal space created by oppressive energies.

"Phantom salt" speaks the deed which never took place but which interrupts their lives in the hoodoo act of breaking a chicken's neck. With their "dream's neck snapped" the Marys are caught in the whirling mix of complaint and grief—complaint against the enormous and singular burden of mother's love and motherwit for God's son, his emissary of flesh to all humanity, alongside their grief over the son's death that religiosity makes more enormous than any heart can bear: "We wait for / his return as shrieking dust."

The cultural voice of the speaker in Jeffers' poem is African American, but this naming is not explicit. The expressive power of the poem is enhanced as Jeffers has avoided limiting its range by showing identity as an entrance. The subtle but distinct cultural references, such as the epigraph which is then repeated, open the ending of the poem to any reader. It is also nonexclusive in gender references inasmuch as the Mary Spirit does not deny her love for her son even as she critiques the world's unsubstantiated reverence for a saint and its unjust disdain for a whore.

The poem is dense to the point of being a pure diamond, suitable—I believe—to the enormous spiritual and historical forces being turned here in a tiny space in time. Much of the success of this poem is this efficient handling of spiritual ethos as large as Judeo-Christian religiosity, a task that might seem unduly ambitious otherwise: "No rolled back stone can dam this grief."

The *Obsidian III* editorial policy (the roman numeral changes with each new editor) has been adjusted to respond to the issue of racial and cultural identity in the creative writing we publish. The year 2000 marked *Obsidian*'s twenty-fifth anniversary, and in that year we decided to open the creative writing of the journal to all writers. The scholarly and critical writing have always been open to all scholars and critics. In the creative writing we are now looking to support a centrality of subject as opposed to a centrality of writers' racial and cultural identities. The subject is *Africana*, or the cultures and lives of people of African descent in the Diaspora, however that may be constructed creatively. We are hoping to encourage a robustness and courage that both embellishes cultural expression and supports the relevance of cultures throughout the African Diaspora to all cultures everywhere. More succinctly, we hope to affirm the human with art.

Honorée Fanonne Jeffers' poem "The Two Marys" is emblematic of *Obsidian III*'s new editorial policy.

Jeffers' poem asks the Mary Spirit to name its Godchild, *"What you gone name that pretty little baby?"* The question is as infinite in the anxiety it produces as it is in the potential grace it can bestow, a grace the two Marys give themselves since they now own this naming space. The poem reveals itself here as supplication, having appealed to its own interior logos and summoned its own answers. These two women raised to mythic dimensions claim the province of their own psyche in a subversion that is subtle, almost imperceptible. Although the ambiguity of the female presence in religiosity is not clearly resolved in the poem (as perhaps it never can be), Jeffers shouts out a harmonic play of spiritual upon gospel that offers eloquence as hope.

"Man prayer bread." The answer is a restructuring of faith, one that is open-ended and positioned against hierarchies.

If you enter from the Hillsborough Street side at North Carolina State University, the *Obsidian* office is located on the second floor in a tiny room lit by the occasional luxury of a shared light from the office across the hallway. From the ground entrance on the rear side of the building you will have another long set of stairs to climb. The twenty-five years gather in this space on the loom and rocking shuttle of an editorial staff that hails from points all over the globe. Each time we initiate the editorial process, seeking to create the next issue, we face the same question.

"What you gone call your gospel?"

Our answer can only be *art*.

Alaska Quarterly Review

Founded 1980

Discovering Something True

by Ronald Spatz

At *Alaska Quarterly Review*, we see our mission as promoting new
and emerging poets and writers. That means we cast our literary
nets as widely as we can and, as a result, the poetry *AQR* publishes
represents a great range of styles and content. Our national repu-
tation is based, in part, upon this eclectic editorial vision. For
some editions I make the final selections, and for other volumes
I call upon a series of diverse and accomplished contributing/
guest poetry editors. Recent poetry editors have included Billy
Collins, Dorianne Laux, Pattiann Rogers, Jane Hirshfield, Stuart
Dybek, Stuart Dischell, and Maxine Kumin. If the poems pub-
lished in *AQR* have certain characteristics, they are these: fresh-
ness, honesty, and a compelling subject. However, there is not al-
ways consensus among our editors about what rises to this level.

What makes a poem stand out to an editor from the hundreds
of other submissions? In my case, the voice of the poem must be
strong–idiosyncratic enough to create a unique persona. But the
answer involves more than that. In keeping with our mission to
publish new poets, I am looking for voices our readers do not
know, voices that may not be reflected in the dominant culture
and that, in all instances, have something important to tell. If I
find such a voice, I will consider the poem seriously.

At the next level of review, I look for the experiential and
revelatory qualities of the poem. I will, without hesitation, cham-

pion a poem that may be less polished or stylistically sophisti-
cated, if the poem engages me, surprises me, and resonates for
me. The joy in reading such a poem is in discovering something
true.

"Adventure in Chinatown 1958" by Susie Silook is a poem
that meets the test for me. One is immediately struck by the
power of Silook's voice. A new writer originally from Gambell
on Alaska's St. Lawrence Island, she uses vivid and yet un-
adorned language that is the perfect complement to her narrative.
She also successfully mixes the conventions of poetry with mem-
oir. Right from the opening line, Silook establishes the
memoiristic tone that contributes to the credibility of the voice.
But her purport is poetic: as Patricia Hampl has observed, the
current interest in memoir "begins not as a reaction to fiction but
as an extension of poetry, the genre our culture claims most to
marginalize." Silook's genre-crossing is especially fitting for her
subject–the cultural survival of a marginalized people.

Adventure in Chinatown 1958

My father was a steel worker in Skokie, Illinois.
    He would leave before dawn and return long after
    the sun no one ever saw in Chicago went down.

My mother says the buildings were too tall and the air
    stank.
    The only place I went was church, she remembers.

My brother Barry was a month old, making me nothing
    but
    a nagging worry in my mother's mind.
    No more babies she thought
    after the third child
    after the fourth child
    after the fifth child
    and the sixth child.

My father's hunting fed his family
    and his mother's family
    and his brother's family.

People still wonder why he agreed to
    the government relocation program and
    without my mother's consent
    to move his Yupik family to Chicago.

In those days they paid the expenses to move
    Native folk out of Native neighborhoods
    and into Asian ones.

It would save them from the mistake
    of the reservation
    would solve the problem
    of that persistent Native identity.

My sister used to take all her clothes off
    and run about naked–
    that's everyone's favorite Chicago story.

My other sister got lost and only spoke Yupik
    and so they took her all over Chinatown
    looking for her non-existent Asian family.

Someone must have told them
    that child is not Asian for
    she remembers eating ice cream at the
    precinct and my father remembers
    how big her eyes were when he
    came to claim his
    relocated but not indigenous to
    Chinatown girl.

Mrs. Silook, why do you want to poison your children?
    the psychiatrist asked my mother.

My father would repeat day in and day out
    Sakuuma paneghaallequusi
    You will all starve if something happens to me.

Finally my Inupiaq-Irish mother who spoke only Yupik
    shouted
    Then we should buy poison and prepare ourselves!

My father wouldn't go to work unless
    she stayed up all night to watch everyone.

The woman was *tired* you got that?

I didn't mean it, she told the lady,
    I was tired of Saavla saying we were going to starve.

So, Custer's Last Stand II
    or infinity
    lasted one month
    in Chinatown.

Better to starve as a Yupik than as an impossible immigrant
    read the fortune cookie of my father
    who says only that
    Chicago is too big to remember.

The poem is set within the context of a United States government relocation program in the 1950s, a program whose goal was assimilation–to place Native Americans in the mainstream and to eliminate their "special status" by "helping" them fit seamlessly into American society. The Silooks were invited to give up their subsistence lifestyle–a harsh and demanding existence in bush Alaska–and to take their place in a great American city. The government promised a good, new life. Here was the chance to trade in the past and its old traditional Yupik ways for the convenience and opportunity of living in the modern world. So, Mr. Silook decided to accept the relocation offer over his wife's objections.

The Silook family was "relocated," but other words come to mind—"hidden" and "disguised." They were sent to a place where they looked like their new neighbors but did not share their neighbors' language, culture, or values. The Silooks' situation was equivalent to dying of cultural thirst. The poet affords us entry into the astonishing experience of an "impossible immigrant," and we are as wide-eyed as her lost Yupik sister in Chinatown.

Silook's authentic voice and the experience of being displaced from one's home and identity are the poem's sources of power. Silook's use of irony and humor—what Grace Paley calls "another kind of light"—to illuminate the racism and cultural genocide inherent in the government's relocation program helps her poem avoid the trap of what could have easily become a didactic, angry tone. Stylistic restraint is key to the poem's success.

Silook conveys the experience of what it is to be "other" in our society. The family fights to stay sane, to hold onto its identity. Against them is the full weight of modern American society, a weight so overwhelming that even years later Mr. Silook can only say, *"Chicago is too big to remember."* The paradox resonates for me every time I read this line.

"Adventure in Chinatown 1958" is a poem that bears witness to the survival of "persistent Native identity" and embodies the triumph of the human spirit, a triumph at the core of what Pablo Neruda said about our inner compass, our greatest strength: "Our original guiding stars are struggle and hope." Silook's work reflects this sense as well as the essential courage poets display when they write what they are *compelled* to write.

A good editor must likewise follow the guiding stars of struggle and hope, as he confronts his magazine's lack of space and so many poems to choose from in service of his readers. My hope is that what I find to be a revelatory experience in a poem will strike a resonant chord with the readers of *Alaska Quarterly Review,* that through our pages readers will experience a world that has been made larger and more meaningful, and that they too will have the joy of discovering something true.

The Women's Review of Books

Founded 1983

On Miriam Goodman's
"Corporate Exercise"

Robin Becker

In her book *Nine Gates: Entering the Mind of Poetry*, Jane Hirshfield
states: "Poems of strong feeling flood, overspill; however much
the poet may have worked them, they taste of the unrestrainable,
of outburst." (NG, p. 23) I like Hirshfield's thesis here for the way
she entangles the highly wrought and technically complex aspects
of prosody with the immediate and emotional body-spirit engine
powering the poem. Like her, I find the "work" of "outburst" en-
gages on several levels, and it's often this juxtaposition that draws
me into a poem. Sometimes a title–punning, out of context, puz-
zling, layered–conveys this multiplicity and I want to investigate.

Corporate Exercise

The room has iron, weights, treadmills, stationary
partners that set part of me in motion.
The floor under my feet, my churning legs, feed back
my performance. They speak to me in fractions of a mile,
sloped to make it harder, calling it a hill. My goal–
to keep the lights lit, the numbers up.
Why must the feedback

count up, like years? Why can't we go backwards?
To zero to youth.
Oh Boss, I am unfit. I lack
your muscle, your thousand-candle-power smile.
Someone in my brain is dreaming; looking at the clock
and counting. I can't hear my pulse for the musical beat.
I live by my ears, more responsive than touch–
the grasshopper mind, the elsewhere heart.
Odd to strip naked for the shower,
when all I want is to armor my body
against the frosty judgment of my peers.

In Goodman's curious title, I fell for the *corporate* with its ety-
mological links to *corporeal, corps,* and *corpus.* In a world of corpo-
rate takeovers and mergers, of universities turning into corpora-
tions, I was eager to see how the word *exercise* played against the
corporate body. My surprise at discovering an actual weight room
(as well as Goodman's mental exercises for surviving one's job in
the corporation) deepened as I read on.

When *stationary* (end word, line one), yields to *motion* (end
word, line two), I'm listening for the poem's rhythm, alert to the
five strong stresses that already characterize the lines. The literal
churning of the speaker's body against the machinery of the gym
suggests that the poem's sounds will reflect and incorporate the
regularity of repetition. Most of the lines contain four or five
strong stresses, with several spilling over to seven and eight.
Goodman's alliteration takes over in the third and fourth lines,
where the *f* sound–a consonant I associate with effort and exer-
tion–dominates the poem in *floor, fleet, feed, performance, fractions.*
Simultaneously, the language of the competitive global market-
place enters the gym with *partners, feedback, performance,* and *goal.*
The speaker has not escaped the corporate job site, where evalu-
ation by peers and superiors determines the quality of work life;
instead, she's internalized and replicated the values and condi-
tions and terms of that world. Her goal remains the same: to keep
"the numbers up."

After the caesura, Goodman asks the question for which there is no answer: "Why can't we go backwards? / To zero to youth." The constant quantifying that permeates "Corporate Exercise" leads the speaker to this imponderable. Overwhelmed by *fractions, goals*, and *numbers*, the poet declares, squarely mid-poem: "Oh Boss, I am unfit. I lack / your muscle, your thousand-candle-power smile." This admission subverts the corporate culture and allows the artist to escape its noose. Part confession, part ironic dodge, the "Oh Boss" names names with a Romantic flourish, conjuring, finally, not the lover/beloved but the plantation manager or prison guard. By employing the double meanings of *unfit* (unsuitable, not in perfect physical condition), Goodman continues the extended metaphor she established in the poem's title. The hard *t* and *k* sounds in *unfit* and *lack* emphasize the speaker's break from the corporate goals. Though she may lack the boss's qualities—business muscle, professional smile—she will dream.

Like women everywhere in untenable situations, the speaker of this poem will retreat, will become "someone in my brain." This divided self is familiar to feminist writers and readers and critics who have, over the last thirty years, reinvigorated images and characters with feminist analysis, transforming withdrawal (or silence) into a stand against the privileging of "muscle." In the gym, pedaling her stationary bike, Goodman's speaker listens to her own "musical beat." She informs us that she will live by her "ears," turning her "grasshopper mind" and "elsewhere heart" away from the "corporate exercise," away from the relentless demands on the body and spirit. A regular iambic line lends closure to the poem, ending the meditation with "against the frosty judgment of my peers." Though the speaker is "naked for the shower," she wants to "armor" her body, protect herself against the corporate enterprise which exacts too high a price for participation.

* * *

Created in response to the mix of silence and misrepresentation of books by and about women, *The Women's Review of Books* provides readers with in-depth reviews on books from a wide range of disciplines. Published monthly (except August), *TWRB* includes in each issue two poems by a single poet. As poetry editor, I read all submissions and select pairs of poems for publication. While our readers are interested in the arts, they are not, for the most part, poets. They come from the sciences, the social sciences; they are historians, lawyers, nurses, and psychologists. They are painters and film makers, technical editors and computer programmers, teachers and booksellers.

In my editorial capacity, I seek poems that explore all aspects of women's lives, and thus I receive work that concerns women's participation in all aspects of art, culture, family, nature, politics, sexuality, sport, work. I am especially interested in poems by underrepresented minorities, lesbians, writers in remote geographic regions, and others disadvantaged or silenced by social mandates. I've published work in translation by writers living in political exile or under dire conditions in their home countries. Beginning writers, midcareer poets, and poets with established reputations submit poetry to our publication. Unpublished, talented writers know they will receive careful consideration, and each year I am proud to introduce the work of six or seven new poets to our readership. Concurrently, I may have poems by Maggie Anderson, Marilyn Hacker, Robin Morgan, and Alicia Ostriker on my desk, and I love the surprise of discovering new work by writers I admire. With its broad readership and interdisciplinary scope, *The Women's Review of Books* offers a unique publishing venue for poets. Where else might 15,000 book-loving nonpoets read a poem?

Mānoa: A Pacific Journal of International Writing

Founded 1988

Courage Borrowed and Out of Bounds

Frank Stewart

Somewhere Rilke says, "Whoever you are, in the evening go outside, out of your room, where you know everything."

When Robbie Shapard and I began *Mānoa* in 1988, our plan was to try something new—to go outside the American literary scene, outside its familiar borders, to places other literary magazines weren't covering very much. We decided to explore the contemporary writing being produced to the west of us, in Asia and the Pacific, and to publish that new writing alongside work by North American authors. We hoped to create a community of international writers and readers from throughout this great blue hemisphere of oceans, islands, and parts of continents, from the North American West to the Asian Far East; from the northern arc of Alaska and Siberia to the southern straits of Indonesia and Chile—and including all the nations of Oceania in between. We were able to take on this project because of the central location of our Honolulu offices, which are as close to Shanghai as to New York, and as close to Tahiti as to Los Angeles. We felt comfortable about being so cosmopolitan in our editorial approach because of the cultural context of our own community, in which for more than a century there has been a mixture of people from the Pacific, Asia, and the Americas.

Because of *Mānoa*'s perspective–looking in a compass direction unfamiliar to mainstream American readers–I knew that the international work we would publish would be challenging on several levels; and I knew we would need to be constantly learning if *Mānoa*'s readers were going to stick with us as we explored what Asian and Pacific writers were doing. But these were all good reasons for starting a new journal. Furthermore, to keep the project lively and even joyful year after year–and because the other editors and I are writers rather than scholars–we determined that the journal would not be "academic"; that is, we would not publish writing that was merely "interesting" but at the same time awful tasting as it went down. This has consistently been our aim in selecting material: that the work be powerful and appealing on its own, and not offered up solely as lessons in culture, geography, ethnicity, style, or politics. Another criterion–and let me speak exclusively about poetry from this point on–has been that the work not be exotic examples and curious artifacts brought back from another world, including the sometimes self-conscious and solipsistic world of American poetic theory. We trusted that having high editorial and production standards, and a different world view from other publications, would enable us to find our audience.

Other general principles for the selection of poetry have been that it be emotionally engaged, surprising, replete, musically sensitive, and carefully made, and that the work produce an illuminative response in the reader that is incommensurate with the sum of all its parts. In short, the same, nearly unattainable qualities that most readers of poetry search for each time they begin a poem. Over the years, we've printed poetry with these qualities from places as various as Papua New Guinea and Korea, translated from such diverse languages as Hawaiian and Chukchi. We've published fine poems composed in the English of such multilingual places as Kuala Lumpur and Manila–and found poetry in the enigmatic landscapes of Idaho and Texas. Often we find ourselves publishing works banned or censored in their home countries, from such nations as Indonesia, China, and Tibet.

Here is a lyric poem by Vietnamese writer Le Thi May, translated by Nguyen Ba Chung, that I think is fairly representative of what *Mānoa* has published:

Wind and Widow

Wind widow willowy
off the arms of dawn and grass
full-chested breath
after so much lovemaking in the night

patches of cloud-clothes discarded in the air
lipstick
sunrise
facial cream
aroma moon of the fourteenth day

wind widow after each makeup
backward glances to another time of sadness and laughter

grass
and dawn rises trembling
separated from wind after lovemaking
all night
. . .
wind elegiac-wind
strands of hair from women who died in the bombing
strands of hair from widows who raised orphaned children
the war after ten years have passed–

"Wind and Widow" appeared in a 1995 *Mānoa* feature on contemporary Vietnamese poetry and prose. The initial gathering and culling was done by American poet and translator Kevin

Bowen; he and I then collaborated to determine the final selection. If I'd received Le Thi May's poem in the mail, separate from any feature we were planning, I might well have printed it on its own. But in this case I was considering a poem knowing that it would appear in a group with other Vietnamese pieces, including two other poems by Le. The feature eventually came to include work by men who had fought in the war, men and women who were born after the war had ended, and younger writers for whom the war was no longer an important literary subject.

While preparing this essay, I asked one of the graduate students working in our office, Lisa Ottiger—a poet in her twenties, and thus a generation younger than I—how she would describe "Wind and Widow." She responded this way:

> This poem at first is strange, surreal; it is also standoffish—it holds you at arm's length until the end. The alliteration of the first line, "Wind widow willowy," and the lack of punctuation make the words run together into one thought: Is the wind willowy, or is the widow? Describing the wind as willowy is strange: you can see mist rising. But then the personification of the landscape is suddenly physical: "arms of dawn and grass / full-chested breath / after so much lovemaking in the night." But are the wind and the earth making love? Or, because there is no one left, is it the wind and the widow making love?
>
> The second stanza juxtaposes images: cloud-clothes, lipstick, sunrise, facial cream. Then the last line brings you to a stop, because it seems that its meaning must be lost in translation: "aroma moon of the fourteenth day." This seems like a folk saying—does it connote fertility? menstrual blood?
>
> In the third stanza the wind and the widow put on makeup, or are they making up? Why does the woman have to paint her face? Who is there to put makeup on for? The first sign that the poem is inhabited by people is the lament in this stanza: "glances to another time of sadness and laughter."
>
> In the fourth stanza, lovemaking seems to result in separation. The ellipsis is mysterious: does it elide the past or the present?
>
> In the last stanza, the wind is an elegy, the wind is the hair of the

dead women and widows raising orphans; and these are the most concrete words in the poem—*bombing, orphaned children, war.*

The last line plays with time: are we looking back at the war, or are we only ten years into it? Are we still at war? The poem whispers, full of ghosts, the elegy of the wind, as if there is no one left.

I would have begun my description of this poem and why it was selected for publication in much the same way. Like Lisa, I'd say that the initial appeal of "Wind and Widow" comes from its mystery and surprises, word by word, starting with the title. *Wind* and *widow*: what do these two words have to do with each other? How can we hold their meanings together in our mind? Is a widow like the wind; is the wind like a widow? If anything, both words are potentially sentimental. And as they draw us into the poem, we expect from such a tenuous beginning that the poem might fail, though we hope that it won't.

With each line, each word and cluster of words, the poem is more perplexing. What are the *arms of dawn*? or *of grass*? The former suggests a familiar personification, Eos, an amorous deity who is also a mistress of Ares, the god of war. And *arms of grass* further suggests both love and death. After we've read the poem a second time, understanding its context as the Vietnam war, *arms* also suggests *armaments,* producing more associations. And then there are the arms of the widows, whose presence grows as the stanzas progress.

In the second stanza, *patches of cloud-clothes discarded in the air* takes us back to those *arms of dawn*—a sense of the out-of-doors world, the clouded dawn sky. But following *after lovemaking all night,* those *cloud-clothes* also suggest a disheveled room, passionate sex, the naked bodies of lovers. And we wonder, When did such lovemaking take place?

And so on, word by word, we ask questions and discover how this poem is an experience in poetic timing, and is also about time—about memory, longing, and being alive in the present while being gathered up in the winds of history and an emotionally intense, individual past. Our eyes and intelligence move from word to word in the poem as the meaning shifts and becomes more subtle. If I were not afraid of tiring the reader, I would discuss how the velocity changes, too, from syllable to syllable, creating with each shift a physical, muscular response in us that almost becomes painful as the poem continues.

But the measured movement and the technical shapeliness of the poem are only two causes of the pleasure we get from it. Just as important, the poem affects us because it verbalizes and makes present real courage in the face of real events–a relationship to the world that is not literary or abstract. By contrast, a great deal of American poetry (and world poetry, for that matter) often does not. Rumi (translated by Coleman Barks) says, "Don't deceive yourself that way! / Having the idea is not living / the reality, of anything. // There's no courage in the idea of battle." Be alive in the real world, he says: "set your heart on this only; the rest is borrowed." Rumi persuades us that poetry is capable of connecting us with one another, with physical experience, and with our interior lives, even as it may simultaneously lift us out of ourselves.

Consciousness and language are intertwined and equally complex, and while they are a large part of what constitutes poetry, we know the world through numerous other means. The brain is not the only thing in nature that thinks, and the best poetry acknowledges that there is a world beyond language, consciousness, and self, as Le's poem does. In "Wind and Widow," the dawn, the grass, the moon, and the wind are all real–not symbols or props–and they exist separately from the speaker (whoever she is), the widow, the other women, the children, and a war that, from 1965 to 1975, created 300,000 orphans and nearly four million deaths.

All of these facts and phenomena exist together, and "Wind and Widow" strives to find meaning in their embrace. Part of the psychic effort being made in Le's poem–an aspect that gives the poem gravity–is its attempt to reconcile human suffering with those things that occupy time and space along with us: elements that live and die, like the grass, and phenomena that seem to come and go, like the phases of the moon, the wind, and war. Le's poem affirms a vision of poetry that is large, and a trust in poetry that allows it to be an instrument through which we can know or at least infer something about such unruly and improbable things as the congruence of matter and emotion. And what's more miraculous, the poem's largeness unfolds within a small, lyrical compass: the intimate rise and fall of a woman's breathing, applying makeup, and making love; and the strands of a widow's hair, blown away in the wind even as they linger season after season.

In editing *Mānoa* I am always looking for work that both honors the art of poetry and acknowledges the risks of the real world. Both are wild with order and disorder beyond measure. And while there are many intelligent and compassionate poets alive today—perhaps more than ever before in history, some of the best of whom are not well known at all—such poems are as hard as ever to write and equally as hard to find. As editor of *Mānoa,* I've been able to look for them not only within the U.S. but in a hemisphere beyond the range of vision of most American readers—outside of that room where, as Rilke says, we know everything.

The Lesbian Review of Books
Founded 1994

Key West Diary: A Search
for a Poetic Tradition

Eloise Klein Healy

As far as poetry editors go at *The Lesbian Review of Books*, I'm the only one. There's no staff or editorial board to help me choose the poems to publish. This fact, in itself, makes for a humbling experience as I think about what the *LRB* is trying to do for lesbian poets and lesbian poetry. When Loralee MacPike started the *LRB* in 1994, she wanted to open up a new space for more and better reviewing of books written by lesbians or books dealing with lesbian issues. She also wanted to give some attention to including poetry in each issue of the review. Loralee and I had worked on many feminist projects together, and so we were familiar with each other's aesthetics and histories as activists and academics. I believe Loralee asked me to be the poetry editor at the *LRB* because I'm small-*c* catholic in my tastes in poetry, and because we share the goal of putting in print the best poems that we can find by lesbian poets.

So, I've "outed" my editorial stance by describing my first rule of thumb: I want to publish really interesting and challenging poems by lesbian poets. The poems don't have to be on a list of topics easily categorized as lesbian: "coming out," love between women, being "butch" or "femme," or espousing a particular political point of view. Not that I haven't published poems that would fall comfortably somewhere on such a list; I just don't go looking for them.

I do go looking for submissions, though. *The Lesbian Review of Books* runs a regular notice stating how and when to submit poems, but I also do a lot of soliciting from people I know and writers whose work I've read in other publications. I also post requests for submissions to some listserves. I want to see lots of poems, and since the *LRB* is primarily a venue for publishing book reviews and not poetry, I feel it is incumbent upon me as a poetry editor to help spread the word about what I'm looking for.

I do receive too many love poems, too many "coming out" poems, too many poems that bemoan the loss of a lover through bad luck, bad timing, and/or bad karma. In short, I see far too many lyrics. If I had it my way, I would see more experimental work, more work in traditional forms, and more translations flooding my mailbox.

The work I've chosen to talk about in this essay moves significantly into territory that really engages me as a poetry editor *and* as a student of both the history of lesbian poets and the developing lesbian literary tradition. *Key West Diary,* a long sequence of poems Pamela Gray wrote about her trip to a conference being held to honor the life and work of Elizabeth Bishop, raises the important problem of the historical invisibility of the lesbian poet and links it to that poet's ongoing personal search for love and relationship. Gray presents a powerful mix of personal and political concerns.

Because of space limitations, I couldn't publish all the twenty-some sections of *Key West Diary* in the *LRB,* so I had to choose the individual poems I felt best represented the underlying themes and overall narrative arc of the whole sequence.

One of the hallmarks of a series or sequence of poems is that it often features musical or dramatic effects that are the result of the poet altering formal qualities and structures from poem to poem. In the case of *Key West Diary,* however, all the works in the sequence are sonnets, though they do not hold to any of the traditional rhyme schemes of sonnets. (There is much internal rhyme, eye-rhyme, and off-rhyme instead.) Selecting which poems to print didn't involve choosing from various kinds of poetic structures. Instead, I had to present the larger story, and it was a challenge to focus on best representing the core of the meaning without sacrificing the range of the work—a poet's multifaceted journey recorded as a diary.

This setup, a diary made of sonnets, attracted me because it mixed categories of writing and levels of formality. The diary is typically viewed as an intimate and personal space, capable of idiosyncratic renderings of experience with no regard for form at all. On the other hand, the sonnet is one of the most rigidly structured traditional forms, with historical precedents governing even topic selection. Gray's playing with these expectations was both part of how her poems worked and what her poems were trying to confront—expectations about identity, quandaries over the meaning or possibility of love, and questions about what she hoped for herself as a woman and a poet.

What was very interesting to me was the nature of the poet's journey through both the present and the past as she sought to know more about Bishop. The poems address Gray's search for a shared lesbian identity with the person and poet Elizabeth Bishop; the poet's search for security in her own relationship with a woman lover who was far away from her physically and emotionally; and, ultimately, the disappointments the poet experienced in these endeavors. Along the way, what I also greatly admired was how Gray paid homage to Bishop's poetry by using a similar vocabulary and echoing the concerns of Bishop's work, particularly her search for "home."

Here are the sections I chose to publish in the *LRB*:

Key West Diary

> The art of losing's not too hard to master,
> though it may look like (*Write* it!) like disaster.
>   –Elizabeth Bishop, "One Art," *Geography III*

i.

I step off a plane not much bigger than
my carry-on bag, into the brightest
sun I've ever seen. I can barely look
at the sky, turquoise as the paua shell
jewelry they sell at Florida gift shops.
It must be close to ninety, sweat dripping
beneath the rose sweater I wore through four
time zones. "America's Caribbean
city... Ninety miles north of Havana..."
In the tiny airport, Bahama fans
do nothing to dispel the heat, cigar
smoke clinging to the humid air. A cab
whisks me past white beaches, date palms,
red mangroves. Alone, I'm here at last.

iv.

Elizabeth Bishop would love the odd
juxtaposition of the engraved gold
plaque on her clapboard Conch house on White Street,
and, alongside it, a red metal sign:
Aqui puede comprar camisetas
Perro. Dog shirts? A Great Dane's picture seems
to imply that. Green shutters, white paint peel-
ing like eggshell, the roof slopes down, juts out–
it's called an "eyebrow house." Bishop planted
the huge pandanu tree in front, largest
on the island, shading the street, dropping
gold coconuts. I picture her, cradling
the root ball, her hands in the dirt, writing
poems in her head, wearing a straw sunhat.

viii.

Elizabeth, I came here for you,
followed the trail of your metaphors
from west to east. It's not a "seminar,"

they say—it's a "poetfest." This wine-red
auditorium is filled with your fans.
Your lover Alice conjures the rainy
Cape Cod afternoon you baked linzertorte,
a poet recalls the blue suit you wore
each week at Harvard, adorned with a pen
like a bent fender. But something's wrong here.
They keep circling around it, the women
in your life were "dear friends," "beloved friends."
Is the word that dangerous? *Lesbian.*
(Say it!) Miss Bishop was a *lesbian.*

    xiii.

At the Southernmost Point in the U.S.,
down the street from the Southernmost Drug Store
and the Southernmost Moped Shop, I stand
on a gray pier above the Atlantic
and try to picture myself on a map,
a speck upon a green island below
Florida's tip. How did I get so far
away? The woman I long for is all
the way across that map and up and up
and up. But it isn't geography
that keeps us apart, and whether I'm south
or north, we still won't find a place where we
can meet each other. From the pier's edge,
I look for Cuba, but see only sky.

This poem addresses the issue of lesbian invisibility head-on.
Rereading Harold Bloom's *The Anxiety of Influence* the other day,
I was reminded that his whole inquiry is possible because there
is a poetic tradition, and there *is* a history studded with stellar
practitioners. If you're a certain kind of young poet looking to join
the conversation, it is very easy to become acquainted with these
practitioners. Pick up any historical anthology of English language
poetry and tick off the names of people you might imitate or steer
clear of.

But if you are another kind of poet, say someone who came of age in the 1960s, '70s, and '80s—the time of "identity politics" and "identity poetics"—searching through a table of contents in *The Norton Anthology of Literature* is not exactly the same as looking in a mirror or a reflecting pool. If you're a woman, a lesbian or gay man, or a person of color, your absence is not news. And a fleshed-out tradition has still not emerged in the present, even with much research on the part of poets and scholars. Thus, I admire Pam Gray for literally getting on the plane and going to that conference. As I've said, I feel one of my goals as an editor is to print poems that reflect attempts to examine/create a lesbian poetic tradition.

I also mentioned that I look for poems that are "off-topic," that enlarge the range of what we might call lesbian poetry. Gray's work paradoxically accomplishes my aim because, although seeking a lesbian tradition is definitely a lesbian topic, she doesn't speak only for her community of identity. Her poems are larger than that. *Key West Diary* opens out to the fact that all writers *hope* to find a community or a forebear with whom to strike up a conversation. For example, look at Gray speaking Bishop's own language from "One Art": Bishop's demand— *"Write* it!" becomes Gray's demand— *"Say* it!"

The problem still remains—nobody is going to "say it" about Bishop.

I like the way Gray uses her poems to issue a challenge, a call to public discourse on the topic. No private whining, please, about how hard it is to be a lesbian poet. Rather, let's talk about how difficult it is to join a conversation in an empty room.

If identity poetics or identity publishing are to make any sense, they must rise above polemic to engage the tradition or lack of it. Gray chose to tackle a member of what, for want of any pre-existing label, I call The Middle Group. They came on the literary scene before the civil rights movement. They were not publicly engaged by early feminism or early lesbian feminism. They wrote in an encoded language. They lived very private lives.

Now we find ourselves a little later in the game, *post-* all these silences. It is time to publish lesbian poems that plant the flags of territorial acquisition and deal with the anxiety of influence in ways yet undefined. I feel the power in this series of "diary entries" comes from Gray's honest search for both herself and the poet Bishop. Gray sets out with many of the questions lesbian poets of my generation have had to ask. Who is the lesbian poet? Where does she come from? As Gray so aptly paints her, a tiny speck backed up against an empty sky, how does she find a name, an address, a home?

I especially like Gray's poems because she chose to pick her fight using a traditional form, one that comes with lots of expectations attached. The sonnet sequence belongs to history—we all know that. But Gray puts it to unconventional uses. As an editor, I look for poetry that is smart enough to use something traditional and make it new, to take on a range of political tasks, and even (I can't believe I'm saying this) to mourn lost love.

Many Mountains Moving
Founded 1994

On Velocity, Mass, and Leaving the Temporal: John Willson's "Morning"

Debra Bokur

An exceptional poem is more than an arrangement of words or a lucky recklessness of imagery—it is, in the truest sense, a portal. For some time now, I have subscribed to the admittedly subjective conviction that the architecture of this portal is secondary to the velocity by which I am propelled beyond its borders. A poet may write of how he has experienced apples or lake water or grief, but for me to be moved by this imagery requires an alchemy unrelated to mere craft. The most technically well-structured poem may remain sadly earthbound, weighted by the unmovable mass of its own self-importance; a good poem removes the reader from the immediate and allows him to view the world with a temporarily altered perception; a great poem remains with the reader, coursing through the veins and changing the pattern of the heart.

I hasten to clarify that despite the above reference to propulsion, I am not an advocate of quick or cursory reading. At *Many Mountains Moving* we receive a phenomenal volume of submissions, each of which our editors read and consider with the same degree of seriousness and respect. And, while outstanding quality is the only criteria by which a work is judged acceptable for publication, the definition of quality is, by default, a matter weighed and determined by this editor, and I must struggle constantly with the degree to which my own world view becomes a factor of judgment.

Our goal at *Many Mountains Moving* is to celebrate a diversity of talents, voices, and visions. To that end, the work must stand alone, unbuoyed and unfettered by strings of academic degrees or publishing credits. After opening an envelope, my first step in the reading process is to slip the cover letter, unread, to the back of the manuscript. If I reach that letter without being captured, without finding the portal, no amount of documented literary expertise will sway me.

John Willson's lyrical "Morning" meets my every expectation for a great poem. It is honest, projecting no sense that the writer is attempting to manipulate my emotions as reader. Its imagery is layered and rich. It has the ability to plunge me beyond that with which I am familiar into one of those welcome rabbit-hole journeys that in the end will prove terrifying, exhausting, and somehow enlightening.

Morning

> There, again, piercing the chatter of other birds,
> a long, single whistle, like a referee's whistle
> stopping play, the bird itself hidden by salal
> and the shadows of madrona and fir. An arrow
> of sound shot back to an alpine dawn: sunlight
>
> through tent fabric turned my hands
> blue as the water where I swam until my eyes
> opened to the same whistle. Creature that stays
> from sight, how do you range from a mountain
> down to this sea-level hawking
> of crows, the finch's gossip?
> Again, your pure syllable

taut as a tent-line from apex to ground.
Did you see the flap open, watch me crawl
out, scoop water to my face,
scratch my chin when glasses
turned a white blob into a goat
above the pass? First-Thing-in-the-Morning,
I have never seen the color of your soft
throat, but with a wingbeat's ease

you shuttle me across the distance, pump
thin air into my lungs, turn me
toward the dwarf lupine by my boot.
Though you remain anonymous as a painter
of ancient caves, I salute you with a cup of tea
and I would welcome your call as the signal,
the last sound before leaving the flesh, the whistle
bearing me into the wild blue.

Though some of Willson's descriptive phrases teeter precari-
ously on the brink of the common, as in "a referee's whistle / stop-
ping play," they also serve as a comfortable point of departure.
The phrase fully serves its purpose, engaging the reader's com-
plete attention. No mere background music, this: indeed, this
same whistle will eventually lead the narrator to contemplate his
own mortality in the poem's final three lines.

The most pervasive theme, and arguably the strongest, is that
of sight: "where I swam until my eyes / opened"; "Creature that
stays / from sight"; "Did you see the flap open, watch me crawl /
out"; "glasses / turned a white blob into a goat"; "I have never
seen the color of your soft / throat." Willson uses the fallibility of
sight to illustrate and acknowledge the limits of our shared human
condition. No matter how acute our vision, we can physically see
no further than this finite sense allows. If, however, we allow our-
selves to be swept beyond the edges of what we know and rec-
ognize, we may begin to see, with the soul's own eye, into that
deeply altered state T.S. Eliot termed "lucid stillness."

The second major theme of "Morning," of course, is that of

birth and death. The narrative line arcs from one to the other with a suppleness of image that lulls me where I sit reading at the window overlooking my aspen grove, then carries me out into a forest I may never see yet can still recognize somewhere deep within my own experience or imagination.

The landscape of birth is clear:

> An arrow
> of sound shot back to an alpine dawn: sunlight
>
> through tent fabric turned my hands
> blue as the water where I swam until my eyes
> opened to the same whistle.

The poet travels through the liquid of some metaphoric birth canal into the light, taking his first breath of the day/his life with a sense of wonder and expectation. Then, birth again: "with a wingbeat's ease // you shuttle me across the distance, pump / thin air into my lungs." And the poet continues to pursue the elusive author of the whistle through the morning toward an acknowledgment of his own inevitable death:

> . . . I would welcome your call as the signal,
> the last sound before leaving the flesh, the whistle
> bearing me into the wild blue.

I am left to consider the circumstances of my own eventual departure from the temporal, and to hope that it may prove equally as sweet.

In marvelous contrast to the familiar image of the referee's whistle, we have such wrenchingly beautiful lines as "An arrow / of sound shot back to an alpine dawn," and "Creature that stays / from sight, how do you range from a mountain / down to this sea-level hawking / of crows, the finch's gossip?" Phrases such as "wingbeat's ease" and "anonymous as a painter / of ancient caves" demonstrate Willson's deftness and descriptive prowess. Thankfully—and refreshingly—the poet escapes the temptation to equate the winged bird with an angel, leaving the reader to draw this conclusion or not. Likewise, he refuses to identify the bird, allowing us to hear whatever call or song holds the most personal significance.

Willson's sparing use of alliteration ("salal / and the shadows"; "taut as a tent-line"; "turn me / toward"; "the signal, / the last sound") makes the device all the more effective. "Morning"'s cadence invites us to read the poem aloud, savoring its phrases.

I remain convinced that one of the greater risks in both life and poetry is succumbing to inertia. I hope to be continually startled, made uncomfortable, and taught. Give me a poem like "Morning," which moves and lifts and makes me believe I have learned the sound that sunlight makes as it sweeps across the forest floor.

Notes on Contributors

David Baker is the poetry editor of *The Kenyon Review*, holds the Thomas B. Fordham Chair of Creative Writing at Denison University, and serves on the faculty of the low-residency MFA program at Warren Wilson College. The most recent of his seven books are *The Truth about Small Towns* (poems, 1999) and *Heresy and the Ideal: On Contemporary Poetry* (essays, 2000).

Robin Becker is the author of five books of poetry, including *The Horse Fair* (2000) and *All-American Girl* (1996), both from the University of Pittsburgh Press; *All-American Girl* won the Lambda Literary Award in Lesbian Poetry. Becker has received fellowships from the Massachusetts Art Foundation, the National Endowment for the Arts, and the Bunting Institute of Radcliffe College. She is the poetry editor of *The Women's Review of Books*.

Debra Bokur, poetry editor of *Many Mountains Moving*, also works out of her Nederland, Colorado, home as a poet and a screenwriter. In the past she has been a film critic, a journalist, a newspaper and magazine editor, and a horse trainer for dressage and three-day eventing. Her own writings have appeared in a variety of national and international magazines, journals, and anthologies.

Hale Chatfield founded the *Hiram Poetry Review* and was its editor from 1967 until his sudden death on Thanksgiving Day, 2000, just as this book was about to go to press. Emeritus Professor of English at Hiram College, where he taught from 1964–1998,

Chatfield's many honors included both a poetry award and an editorial excellence award from the Ohioana Library Association. He was also president of Chatfield Software, Inc., designers and distributors of computer software.

Peter Cooley was born in Detroit, growing up there and in the city suburbs. A graduate of Shimer College, the University of Chicago, and the University of Iowa, he is currently professor of English at Tulane University. Of Cooley's six books of poetry, five—*The Room Where Summer Ends, Night Seasons, The Van Gogh Notebooks, The Astonished Hours,* and *Sacred Conversations*—were published by Carnegie Mellon University Press. He was poetry editor of *The North American Review* for thirty years, stepping down in late 2000 following the retirement of long-time editor-in-chief Robley Wilson.

George Core, who has edited *The Sewanee Review* at The University of the South since 1973, is a frequent contributor to such periodicals as *Book World, The Virginia Quarterly Review,* and *The Hudson Review.*

Stephen Corey is associate editor of *The Georgia Review*, with which he has worked since 1983; from 1977–1983 co-edited and then edited *The Devil's Millhopper*, an independent poetry magazine. He has published eight poetry collections, most recently *Mortal Fathers and Daughters* (Palanquin Press, 1999) and *Greatest Hits, 1980–2000* (Pudding House Press, 2000). His essays, articles, and reviews have appeared in numerous literary magazines over the past twenty-five years.

Richard Foerster has worked on the staff of *Chelsea* since 1974, becoming its editor in 1994. Among his three books of poems are *Sudden Harbor* and *Patterns of Descent* from Orchises Press and *Trillium* (1998) from BOA Editions—which will bring out his fourth collection, *Double Going*, early in 2002. Recipient of a Discovery/ *The Nation* Award, fellowships from the NEA and the Maine Arts

Commission, and (for 2000–20001) an Amy Lowell Travelling Scholarship, Foerster lives in Maine and works as a freelance type-setter for small literary presses.

David Hamilton has been the editor of *The Iowa Review* for over twenty years. Otherwise, he is at least a part-time medievalist, teaching Chaucer and the medieval lyric fairly regularly at the University of Iowa. His essays have appeared in *The North Dakota Quarterly, The Gettysburg Review,* and *A Place of Sense: Searching for the Midwest,* edited by Michael Martone.

Eloise Klein Healy is the founding chair of the MFA in Creative Writing Program at Antioch University in Los Angeles and associate editor/poetry editor of *The Lesbian Review of Books.* Her four collections of poetry include *Women's Studies Chronicles* (The Inevitable Press, 1998) and *Artemis in Echo Park* (Firebrand Books, 2000); her poems have also appeared in such anthologies as *The World in Us: Lesbian and Gay Poetry of the Next Wave* and *The Geography of Home: California's Poetry of Place.*

Warren Slesinger is the editor and publisher of The Bench Press. He has taught creative writing part time while working full time in the publishing business as, variously, an editor, marketing manager, and sales manager for the university presses of Chicago, Oregon, Pennsylvania, and South Carolina. His poems have appeared in numerous literary magazines through the years.

Dave Smith is co-editor of *The Southern Review* and Boyd Professor of English at Louisiana State University. His numerous poetry collections include *The Wick of Memory: New and Selected Poems 1970–2000* (LSU Press, 2000).

R. T. Smith, editor of Washington and Lee University's *Shenandoah* since 1995, was at various times founding editor of *Cold Mountain Review,* co-editor of *Southern Humanities Review,* and poetry editor of *National Forum.* He has published nine books of poems, among them the recently released *Split the Lark: Selected Poems* (Salmon Press) and *Messenger* (Louisiana State University Press).

Ronald Spatz, founding and executive editor of *Alaska Quarterly Review*, is also chair of the creative writing department and director of the honors program at the University of Alaska at Anchorage. His writing has earned fellowships from the NEA and the Alaska State Council on the Arts, and he has also produced and directed some short films–including *For the Love of Ben*, nationally broadcast on public television.

Frank Stewart is editor of *Mānoa* and teaches at the University of Hawai'i in Honolulu. He is a poet, translator, and essayist who has published ten books, including three of poetry, and who is a past recipient of the Whiting Award.

Robert Stewart teaches in the Professional Writing Program at the University of Missouri-Kansas City, where he is managing editor of *New Letters* magazine and associate producer for the *New Letters on the Air* radio series. His poetry collections include *Plumbers* (BkMk Press, 1988), *Letter from the Living* (Borderline Editions, 1992), and three chapbooks. He has edited numerous anthologies of poetry and essays, including the forthcoming *Spud Songs: Potato Poems*, a book to benefit hunger relief.

Marion Stocking has been an editor of *The Beloit Poetry Journal* since 1954, the year she joined the English department of Beloit College in Wisconsin. Her scholarly publications on the Byron/ Shelley circle have won national and international awards; she has edited *A Fine Excess* (2000), an anthology of poems from the magazine's first fifty years, as well as a collection of her own book reviews. Stocking has lived in Maine since her retirement from Beloit College.

William Trowbridge, Distinguished University Professor Emeritus at Northwest Missouri State University, served for fourteen years as co-editor of *The Laurel Review* at NMSU. His poetry publications include three full-length collections from the University of Arkansas Press—*Flickers* (2000), *O Paradise* (1995), and *Enter Dark Stranger* (1989)—and a chapbook from Iowa State University Press, *The Book of Kong* (1986), which has just been reissued in an online version by Small Mouth Press.

Afaa Michael Weaver, poet and playwright, is editor of *Obsidian III* and Alumnae Professor of English at Simmons College in Boston. His *Multitudes: Poems New and Selected* (2000) was published by Sarabande Books; earlier collections include *Talisman* (1998) and *Stations in a Dream* (1993). A veteran of fifteen years as a blue-collar factory worker in his native Baltimore, Weaver holds an MFA from Brown University.

Christopher J. Windolph is a teaching fellow and graduate student majoring in early American literature at the University of North Carolina at Chapel Hill, where he is writing a dissertation on geometry and American romanticism. He has served on the editorial board of *The Carolina Quarterly* for four years; in 1998 he was poetry co-editor, and in 1999 he became poetry editor.

John Witte is a poet and teacher as well as the editor of *Northwest Review*. His poems have appeared in such publications as *The New Yorker* and *The Paris Review*; his collection *Loving the Days* is available from Wesleyan University Press, and he has edited *The Collected Poems of Hazel Hall* for Oregon State University Press. He has been the recipient of numerous grants, including two fellowships from the National Endowment for the Arts.

Index of Magazines with Addresses

Alaska Quarterly Review
University of Alaska
3211 Providence Drive
Anchorage, AK 99508

The Beloit Poetry Journal
Box 154, RFD 2
Ellsworth, ME 04605

The Carolina Quarterly
Greenlaw Hall CB #3520
University of North Carolina
Chapel Hill, NC 27599–3520

Chelsea
Box 773
Cooper Station, NY 10276–0773

The Georgia Review
012 Gilbert Hall
University of Georgia
Athens, GA 30602–9009

Hiram Poetry Review
Box 162
Hiram, Ohio 44234

The Iowa Review
308 EPB
University of Iowa
Iowa City, Iowa 52242

The Kenyon Review
Kenyon College
Gambier, Ohio 43022

The Laurel Review
Greentower Press
Department of English
Northwest Missouri State University
Maryville, MO 64468

The Lesbian Review of Books
4350 Allot Avenue
Sherman Oaks, CA 91423

Mānoa: A Pacific Journal of International Writing
English Department
University of Hawaii
Honolulu, HI 96822

Many Mountains Moving
1 22nd Street
Boulder, CO 80302

New Letters
University of Missouri
Kansas City, MO 64110

The North American Review
University of Northern Iowa
Cedar Falls, IA 50614

The Northwest Review
369 PLC
University of Oregon
Eugene, OR 97403

Obsidian III
Box 8105
Department of English
North Carolina State University
Raleigh, NC 27695

The Sewanee Review
University of the South
Sewanee, TN 37375

Shenandoah
Troubadour Theatre, 2nd Floor
Washington & Lee University
Lexington, VA 24450

The Southern Review
43 Allen Hall
Louisiana State University
Baton Rouge. LA 70803

The Women's Review of Books
Wellesley College Center for Research on Women
Wellesley , MA 02481

Index of Poets and Poems